curriculum mathematics practice

answers

C Oliver   **A Ledsham**   **R Elvin**   **M Bindley**

Oxford University Press

Oxford University Press, Great Clarendon Street, Oxford OX2 6DP

Oxford   New York
Athens   Auckland   Bangkok   Bogota   Bombay
Buenos Aires   Calcutta   Cape Town   Dar es Salaam   Delhi
Florence   Hong Kong   Istanbul   Karachi   Kuala Lumpur
Madras   Madrid   Melbourne   Mexico City   Nairobi
Paris   Singapore   Taipei   Tokyo   Toronto

and associated companies in

Berlin Ibadan

Oxford is a trade mark of Oxford University Press
© Oxford University Press 1996

Series first published as *Comprehensive Mathematics Practice* 1981
Updated edition of *Curriculum Mathematics Practice* first published 1996

Reprinted 1997

ISBN 0 19 833747 7
A CIP record for this book is available from the British Library.

Typeset and illustrated by Tech Set Ltd
Printed and bound in Hong Kong

Preface

Curriculum Mathematics Practice is an updated version of *Comprehensive Mathematics Practice*, a successful series designed for the majority of students in their first years of secondary schooling. As before, the books provide a vast range of carefully constructed and graded exercises in a coherent mathematical progression, with many of these exercises set in a real-life context. The levels targeted are 3–8, and details of how all six new books relate to the curriculum are given in the Answer Book.

These new books do not attempt to provide a complete scheme for the National Curriculum. No attempt has been made for instance to cover 'Using and Applying Mathematics' or computer work. It is expected, however, that mathematics departments will use other resources for those aspects (e.g. *Oxford Mathematics*) and that *Curriculum Mathematics Practice* will provide a core of skill practice within an overall scheme of work.

The series has the same objective as the original books. The series should enable students 'to gain confidence in their abilities and master the fundamental processes so necessary for future success'.

Mark Bindley
Revising Editor
December 1995

Contents

Summary of coverage of National Curriculum in *Curriculum Mathematics Practice* Books 1–6

NATIONAL CURRICULUM REFERENCING

The referencing covers Levels 3 to 8 of these Attainment Targets in the 1995 National Curriculum Document.

AT 2   Number and Algebra
AT 3   Shape, Space and Measures
AT 4   Handling Data

Each Level Description within these Attainment Targets consists of a prose paragraph containing several, often unrelated, statements of attainment.
In this referencing system the statements within each level have been numbered.
For example:

AT 2/3 (ii) refers to AT 2 (Number and algebra), Level 3 statement (ii)
AT 3/4 (vii) refers to AT 3 (Shape, space and measures), Level 4, statement (vii)

Number and algebra

AT 2/3 (i)   Pupils show understanding of place value in numbers up to 1000 and use this to make approximations.
Book 1, Unit 1

AT 2/3 (ii) (part)   Pupils have begun to use decimal notation in contexts such as money, temperature and calculator displays.
Book 2, Unit 1

AT 2/3 (ii) (part)   Pupils have begun to recognise negative numbers in contexts such as money, temperature and calculator displays.
Book 3, Unit 1

AT 2/3 (iii)   Pupils use mental recall of addition and subtraction facts to 20 in solving problems involving larger numbers.
Book 1, Unit 3

AT 2/3 (iv)   Pupils use mental recall of the 2, 5 and 10 multiplication tables, and others up to 5×5, in solving whole-number problems involving multiplication and division, including those that give rise to remainders. Puils use calculator methods where numbers include several digits.
Book 1, Unit 5

AT 2/3 (v)   Pupils have begun to develop mental strategies, and use them to find methods for adding and subtracting numbers with at least two digits.
Book 1, Units 3, 9

AT 2/4 (i)   Pupils use their understanding of place value to multiply and divide whole numbers by 10 or 100.
Book 1, Unit 1

AT 2/4 (ii)   In solving number problems, pupils use a range of mental and written methods of computation with the four operations, including mental recall of multiplication facts up to 10×10.
Book 1, Unit 9

AT 2/4 (iii)   Pupils add and subtract decimals to two places.
Book 2, Unit 1

AT 2/4 (iv)   In solving problems with or without a calculator, pupils check the reasonableness of their results by reference to their knowledge of the context or to the size of the numbers.
Book 1, Unit 9

AT 2/4 (v)   Pupils recognise approximate proportions of a whole and use simple fractions and percentages to describe these.
Book 2, Unit 4

AT 2/4 (vi)   Pupils explore and describe number patterns, and relationships including multiple, factor and square.
Book 1, Unit 7

AT 2/4 (vii)   Pupils have begun to use simple formulae expressed in words.
Book 2, Unit 5

AT 2/4 (viii)   Pupils use and interpret co-ordinates in the first quadrant.
Book 2, Unit 7

AT 2/5 (i)   Pupils use their understanding of place value to multiply and divide whole numbers and decimals by 10, 100 and 1000.
Book 2, Unit 1

AT 2/5 (ii)   Pupils order, add and subtract negative numbers in context.
Book 3, Unit 1

AT 2.5 (ii)   Pupils use all four operations with decimals in two places.
Book 3, Unit 2

AT 2/5 (iv)   Pupils calculate fractional or percentage parts of quantities and measurements, using a calculator where appropriate.
Book 3, Unit 5

AT 2/5 (v)   Pupils understand and use an appropriate non-calculator method for solving problems that involve multiplying and dividing any three-digit number by any two-digit number.
Book 1, Unit 9

AT 2/5 (vi)   Pupils check their solutions by applying inverse operations or estimating using approximations.
Book 1, Unit 9

AT 2/5 (vii)   Pupils construct, express in symbolic form, and use simple formulae involving one or two operations.
Book 2, Unit 5

AT 2/6 (i)   Pupils order and approximate decimals when solving numerical problems and equations such as $x^2 = 20$, using trial-and-improvement methods.
Book 3, Unit 2

AT 2/6 (ii)   Pupils are aware of which number to consider as 100 per cent, or a whole, in problems involving comparisons, and use this to evaluate one number as a fraction or percentage of another.
Book 3, Unit 5

AT 2/6 (iii)   Pupils understand and use the equivalences between fractions, decimals and percentages.
Book 2, Unit 4

AT 2/6 (iv)   Pupils calculate using ratio in appropriate situations.
Book 4, Unit 1

AT 2/6 (v)   When exploring number patterns, pupils find and describe in words the rule for the next term or nth term of a sequence where the rule is linear.
Book 4, Unit 3

AT 2/6 (vi)   Pupils formulate and solve linear equations with whole-number coefficients.
Book 4, Unit 5

AT 2/6 (vii)   Pupils represent mappings expressed algebraically, interpreting general features and using graphical representation in four quadrants where appropriate.
Book 4, Unit 8

AT 2/7 (i)   In making estimates, pupils round to one significant figure and multiply and divide mentally.
Book 3, Unit 2

AT 2/7 (ii)   Pupils understand the effects of multiplying and dividing by numbers between 0 and 1.
Book 5, Unit 6

AT 2/7 (iii)   Pupils solve numerical problems involving multiplication and division with numbers of any size, using a calculator efficiently and appropriately.
Book 1, Units 1, 3, 5, 7, 9

AT 2/7 (iv)   Pupils understand and use proportional changes.
Book 5, Unit 6

AT 2/7 (v)   Pupils find and describe in symbols the next term or nth term of a sequence where the rule is quadratic.
Book 4, Unit 3

AT 2/7 (vi)   Pupils use algebraic and graphical methods to solve simultaneous linear equations in two variables.
Book 5, Unit 7

AT 2/7 (vii)   Pupils solve simple inequalities.
Book 4, Unit 5

AT 2/8 (i)   Pupils solve problems involving calculating with powers, roots and numbers expressed in standard form, checking for the correct order of magnitude.
Book 6, Unit 1

AT 2/8 (ii)   Pupils choose to use fractions or percentages to solve problems involving repeated proportional changes or the calculation of the original quantity given the result of a proportional change.
Book 5, Unit 6; Book 6, Unit 1

AT 2/8 (iii)   Pupils evaluate algebraic formulae, substituting fractions, decimals and negative numbers. They calculate one variable, given the others, in formulae such as $V = \pi r^2 h$.
Book 6, Unit 2

AT 2/8 (iv)	Pupils manipulate algebraic formulae, equations and expressions, finding common factors and multiplying two linear expressions. *Book 6, Unit 2*	**AT 2/8 (vii)**	Pupils sketch and interpret graphs of linear, quadratic, cubic and reciprocal functions, and graphs that model real situations. *Book 8, Unit 4*
AT 2/8 (vi)	Pupils solve inequalities in two variables. *Book 5, Unit 7*		

Shape, space and measures

AT 3/3 (i)	Pupils classify 3-D and 2-D shapes in various ways, using mathematical properties such as reflective symmetry. *Book 1, Unit 2*	**AT 3/5 (i)**	When constructing models and when drawing or using shapes, pupils measure and draw angles to the nearest degree, and use language associated with angle. *Book 3, Unit 6*
AT 3.3 (ii)	Pupils use non-standard units and standard metric units of length, capacity, mass and time, in a range of contexts. *Book 2, Unit 6; Book 1, Unit 4*	**AT 3/5 (ii)**	Pupils identify all the symmetries of 2-D shapes. *Book 2, Unit 3*
AT 3/4 (i)	Pupils make 3-D mathematical models by linking given faces or edges. *Book 1, Unit 6*	**AT 3/5 (iii)**	Pupils know the rough metric equivalents of Imperial units still in daily use and convert one metric unit to make another. They make sensible estimates of a range of measures in relation to everyday situations. *Book 2, Unit 6*
AT 3/4 (ii)	Pupils draw common 3-D shapes in different orientations on grids. *Book 3, Unit 3*		
AT 3/4 (iii)	Pupils identify congruent shapes. *Book 3, Unit 3*	**AT 3/5 (iv)**	From programme of study **3b** pupils should be taught to recognise and visualise the transformations of translation, reflection, rotation and enlargement, and their combination in two dimensions; understand the notations used to describe them. *Book 2, Unit 3*
AT 3/4 (iv)	Pupils identify orders of rotational symmetry. *Book 2, Unit 3*		
AT 3/4 (v)	Pupils reflect simple shapes in a mirror line. *Book 1, Unit 2*		
AT 3/4 (vi)	Pupils choose and use appropriate units and instruments, interpreting, with appropriate accuracy, numbers on a range of measuring instruments. *Book 2, Unit 6; Book 3, Unit 6*	**AT 3/6 (i)**	Pupils recognise and use common 2-D representations of 3-D objects. *Book 4, Unit 6*
		AT 3/6 (ii)	Pupils know and use the proprties of quadrilaterals in classifying different types of quadrilateral. They solve problems using angle and symmetry properties of intersecting and parallel lines, and explain these properties. *Book 4, Unit 2*
AT 3/4 (vii)	Pupils find perimeters of simple shapes, find areas by counting squares, and find volumes by counting cubes. *Book 2, Unit 2*		

AT 3/6 (iii)	Pupils devise instructions for a computer to generate and transform shapes and paths. *Not covered*	AT 3/7 (iii)	Pupils enlarge shapes by a fractional scale factor. *Book 5, Unit 2*
AT 3/6 (iv)	Pupils understand and use appropriate formulae for finding the areas of plane rectilinear figures. *Book 4, Unit 4*	AT 3/7 (iv)	Pupils determine the locus of an object moving according to a rule. *Book 5, Unit 5*
AT 3/6 (v)	Pupils understand and use appropriate formulae for finding the circumferences and areas of circles. *Book 5, Unit 4*	AT 3/7 (v)	Pupils appreciate the continuous nature of measurement and recognise that a measurement given to the nearest whole number may be inaccurate by up to one half in either direction. *Book 3, Unit 2*
AT 3/6 (vi)	Pupils understand and use appropriate formulae for finding the volumes of cuboids. *Book 5, Unit 4*	AT 3/7 (vi)	Pupils understand and use compound measures, such as speed. *Book 3, Unit 2*
AT 3/6 (vii)	Pupils enlarge shapes by a positive whole-number scale factor. *Book 5, Unit 2*	AT 3/8 (i)	Pupils understand and use mathematical similarity. *Book 5, Unit 2*
AT 3/7 (i)	Pupils understand and apply Pythagoras' theorem when solving problems in two dimensions. *Book 5, Unit 1*	AT 3/8 (i)	Pupils use sine, cosine and tangent in right-angled triangles when solving problems in two dimensions. *Book 6, Unit 5*
AT 3/7 (ii)	Pupils calculate lengths, areas and volumes in plane shapes and right prisms. *Book 5, Unit 4*	AT 3/8 (iii)	Pupils distinguish between formulae for perimeter, area and volume by considering dimensions. *Book 5, Unit 4*

Handling data

AT 4/3 (i)	Pupils extract and interpret information presented in simple tables and lists. *Book 1, Unit 4*	AT 4/4 (iii)	Pupils group data, where appropriate, in equal class intervals, represent collected data in frequency diagrams and interpret such diagrams. *Book 1, Unit 8*
AT 4/3 (ii)	Pupils construct bar charts and pictograms, where the symbol represents a group of units, to communicate information they have gathered, and they interpret information presented to them in these forms. *Book 1, Unit 8*	AT 4/4 (iv)	Pupils construct and interpret simple line graphs. *Book 3, Unit 4*
AT 4/4 (i)	Pupils collect discrete data and record them using a frequency table. *Book 1, Unit 8*	AT 4/4 (v)	Pupils understand and use simple vocabulary associated with probability, including 'fair', 'certain' and 'likely'. *Book 3, Unit 7*
AT 4/4 (ii)	Pupils understand and use the mode and the median. *Book 2, Unit 8*	AT 4/5 (i)	Pupils understand and use the mean of discrete data. *Book 2, Unit 8*

AT 4/5 (ii)   Pupils compare two simple distributions, using the range and one of the measures of average.
Book 3, Unit 8; Book 2, Unit 8

AT 4/5 (iii)   Pupils interpret graphs and diagrams, including pie charts, and draw conclusions.
Book 3, Unit 8

AT 4/5 (iv)   Pupils understand and use the probability scale from 0 to 1.
Book 3, Unit 7

AT 4/5 (v)   Pupils find and justify probabilities, and approximations to these, by selecting and using methods based on equally likely outcomes and experimental evidence, as appropriate. They understand that different outcomes may result from repeating an experiment.
Book 3, Unit 7

AT 4/6 (i)   Pupils collect and record continuous data, choosing appropriate equal class intervals over a sensible range to create frequency tables.
Book 5, Unit 3

AT 4/6 (ii)   Pupils construct and interpret frequency diagrams.
Book 5, Unit 3

AT 4/6 (iii)   Pupils construct pie charts.
Book 3, Unit 8

AT 4/6 (iv)   Pupils draw conclusions from scatter diagrams, and have a basic understanding of correlation.
Book 4, Unity 9

AT 4/6 (v)   When dealing with a combination of two experiments, pupils identify all the outcomes, using diagrammatic, tabular or other forms of communication.
Book 4, Unit 7

AT 4/6 (vi)   In solving problems, pupils use their knowledge that the total probability of all mutually exclusive outcomes of an experiment is 1.
Book 4, Unit 7

AT 4/7 (i)   Pupils specify hypotheses and test them by designing and using appropriate methods that take account of bias.
Not covered

AT 4/7 (ii)   Pupils determine the modal class and estimate the mean, median and range of sets of grouped data, selecting the statistic most appropriate to their line of enquiry.
Book 5, Unit 3

AT 4/7 (iii)   Pupils use measures of average and range, with associated frequency polygons, as appropriate, to compare distributions and make inferences.
Book 5, Unit 3

AT 4/7 (iv)   Pupils use measures of average and range, with associated frequency polygons, as appropriate, to compare distributions and make inferences.
Book 5, Unit 3

AT 4/7 (v)   Pupils understand relative frequency as an estimate of probability and use this to compare outcomes of experiments.
Book 4, Unit 7

AT 4/8 (i)   Pupils interpret and construct cumulative frequency tables and diagrams, using the upper boundary of the class interval.
Book 5, Unit 3

AT 4.8 (ii)   Pupils estimate the median and interquartile range and use these to compare distributions and make inferences.
Book 5, Unit 3

AT 4/8 (iii)   Pupils understand when to apply methods for calculating the probability of a compound event, given the probabilities of either independent events or mutually exclusive events; they use these methods appropriately in solving problems.
Book 6, Unit 3

Book 1 Unit 1

| AT 2/3 (i) | Pupils show understanding of place value in numbers up to 1000 and use this to make approximations. |
| AT 2/4 (i) | Pupils use their understanding of place value to multiply and divide whole numbers by 10 or 100. |

Exercise 1.1 *page 1*

1 twelve   2 fifteen   3 thirty-six   4 ninety-one
5 one hundred and fifty   6 three hundred and forty
7 three hundred and forty-five   8 two hundred and ten
9 two hundred and seventeen   10 five hundred and eight
11 six hundred and one   12 two thousand three hundred
13 two thousand three hundred and seventy
14 three thousand six hundred and seventy
15 three thousand six hundred and seventy-eight
16 seven thousand two hundred and ten
17 seven thousand two hundred and fifteen
18 seven thousand two hundred and three
19 four thousand five hundred and four
20 four thousand and twenty-four   21 three thousand and thirty-seven
22 three thousand and thirty   23 eight thousand and twenty
24 eight thousand and seven   25 nine thousand and one
26 **a** three hundred and nine metres
   b eighty-three kilometres
   c five hundred and fifty-nine kilometres
27 two thousand four hundred and fourteen metres
28 **a** four thousand eight hundred and fifty-seven kilometres
   b seven thousand two hundred and seventy kilometres
   c nine thousand five hundred and fifteen kilometres

Exercise 1.2 *page 1*

1 17	2 19	3 45	4 73	5 190	6 460
7 467	8 810	9 812	10 704	11 901	12 6500
13 6520	14 9130	15 9133	16 3610	17 3619	18 3602
19 8706	20 8091	21 1056	22 1050	23 4010	24 4004
25 8011	26 736	27 887	28 9121	29 7206	30 1085

Exercise 1.3 *page 2*

1 1	2 6	3 5	4 3	5 7	6 30
7 50	8 300	9 900	10 500	11 6	12 2
13 7	14 2	15 70	16 10	17 60	18 50
19 900	20 100	21 300	22 200	23 8000	24 1000
25 9000					

Exercise 1.4 *page 2*

1 70, 71, 72, 73, 75	**2** 40, 45, 50, 54, 55
3 112, 113, 121, 123, 132	**4** 99, 109, 110, 112, 120
5 412, 421, 423, 432, 433	**6** 504, 505, 530, 534, 540
7 678, 687, 768, 786, 876	**8** 2123, 2132, 2231, 2312, 2321
9 1006, 1016, 1060, 1061, 1106	**10** 4004, 4040, 4044, 4400, 4404
11 88, 89, 90, 98, 99	**12** 80, 88, 108, 118, 180
13 103, 113, 123, 130, 133	**14** 215, 220, 225, 250, 255
15 605, 606, 650, 660, 665	**16** 56, 55, 54, 45, 44
17 119, 109, 104, 99, 94	**18** 155, 150, 125, 120, 105
19 352, 350, 342, 332, 330	**20** 444, 441, 440, 414, 404

Exercise 1.5 *page 3*

1 532, 235	**2** 943, 349	**3** 861, 168	**4** 553, 355
5 760, 607	**6** 6543, 3456	**7** 9741, 1479	**8** 8521, 1258
9 7511, 1157	**10** 6633, 3366	**11** 5320, 2035	**12** 9700, 7009

Exercise 1.6 *page 3*

1 40	**2** 70	**3** 150	**4** 190	**5** 100	**6** 240
7 430	**8** 520	**9** 690	**10** 200	**11** 500	**12** 1260
13 1550	**14** 3170	**15** 6320	**16** 5100	**17** 8500	**18** 7000
19 23 170	**20** 35 470	**21** 46 200	**22** 70 500	**23** 53 000	**24** 80 000
25 99 010					

Exercise 1.7 *page 3*

1 3	**2** 5	**3** 7	**4** 6 r 5	**5** 5 r 4	**6** 7 r 3
7 12	**8** 16	**9** 37	**10** 82	**11** 20	**12** 90
13 44 r 5	**14** 63 r 8	**15** 30 r 7	**16** 40 r 2	**17** 132	**18** 478
19 230	**20** 520	**21** 700	**22** 517 r 6	**23** 307 r 8	**24** 420 r 4
25 900 r 1					

Exercise 1.8 *page 3*

1 300	**2** 900	**3** 1300	**4** 1600	**5** 1000	**6** 2500
7 5100	**8** 7800	**9** 3000	**10** 6000	**11** 12 400	**12** 23 700
13 51 900	**14** 70 800	**15** 63 000	**16** 81 000	**17** 40 000	**18** 90 000
19 10 000	**20** 99 900				

Exercise 1.9 *page 3*

1 2	**2** 6	**3** 8	**4** 8 r 50	**5** 8 r 53	**6** 7 r 64
7 7 r 4	**8** 5 r 2	**9** 32	**10** 97	**11** 97 r 10	**12** 46 r 80
13 46 r 83	**14** 51 r 62	**15** 93 r 75	**16** 41 r 18	**17** 13 r 84	**18** 37 r 25
19 37 r 5	**20** 51 r 7	**21** 50 r 7	**22** 20 r 8	**23** 20 r 30	**24** 80 r 70

Exercise 1.10 *page 4*

1 £540	**2** 200 cm, 2 m	**3** 9500 cm, 95 m
4 a 12 **b** 5	**5 a** 13 **b** 18	

Exercise 1.11 *page 4*

1, 2 and **3** $26 \times 10 = 260$	**4, 5** and **6** $260 \div 10 = 26$
7, 8 and **9** $70 \times 10 = 700$	**10, 11** and **12** $700 \div 10 = 70$
13, 14 and **15** $145 \times 10 = 1450$	**16, 17** and **18** $1450 \div 10 = 145$
19, 20 and **21** $240 \times 10 = 2400$	**22, 23** and **24** $2400 \div 10 = 240$
25, 26 and **27** $400 \times 10 = 4000$	**28, 29** and **30** $4000 \div 10 = 400$
31, 32 and **33** $13 \times 100 = 1300$	**34, 35** and **36** $1300 \div 100 = 13$
37, 38 and **39** $50 \times 100 = 5000$	**40, 41** and **42** $5000 \div 100 = 50$

Exercise 1.12 *page 5*

1 30	**2** 50	**3** 50	**4** 80	**5** 20	**6** 90
7 90	**8** 20	**9** 10	**10** 70	**11** 40	**12** 100
13 170	**14** 150	**15** 150	**16** 320	**17** 540	**18** 280
19 110	**20** 610	**21** 470	**22** 100	**23** 200	**24** 190
25 310			**26 a** 200	**b** 400	**c** 500

27	a	300	b	600	c	700	28	a	100	b	300	c	500
29	a	300	b	400	c	700	30	a	200	b	100	c	500
31	a	700	b	900	c	500	32	a	600	b	700	c	1000
33	a	900	b	800	c	500	34	a	900	b	800	c	600
35	a	100	b	200	c	300							

36	1640	37	3480	38	7280	39	2850	40	4560	41	6730
42	1600	43	5100	44	1900	45	7400	46	5400	47	2700
48	6200	49	3300	50	3000	51	2000	52	3000	53	3000
54	6000	55	5000	56	9000	57	6000				

58	a	1690	b	1700	c	2000	59	a	3480	b	3500	c	3000
60	a	2140	b	2100	c	2000	61	a	4310	b	4300	c	4000
62	a	3720	b	3700	c	4000	63	a	5860	b	5900	c	6000
64	a	2570	b	2600	c	3000	65	a	1360	b	1400	c	1000
66	a	7430	b	7400	c	7000	67	a	2610	b	2600	c	3000
68	a	3800	b	3800	c	4000	69	a	4080	b	4100	c	4000
70	a	8030	b	8000	c	8000							

Book 1 Unit 2

AT 3/3 (i)	Pupils classify 3-D and 2-D shapes in a variety of ways, using mathematical properties such as reflective symmetry.
AT 3/4 (v)	Pupils reflect simple shapes in a mirror line.

Exercise 2.1 *page 6*

1 b	2 a	3 c	4 a	5 a	6 b

Exercise 2.2 *page 9*

1 b	2 c	3 b	4 d	5 c	6 a

Exercise 2.3 *page 12*

1 b	2 a	3 a	4 b	5 c	6 b

Book 1 Unit 3

AT 2/3 (iii)	Pupils use mental recall of addition and subtraction facts to 20 in solving problems involving larger numbers.
AT 2/3 (v)	Pupils have begun to develop mental strategies, and use them to find methods for adding and subtracting numberts with at least two digits.

Exercise 3.1 *page 21*

1 c	2 d	3 b	4 a	5 b	6 c	7 b	8 c
9 c	10 a	11 d	12 c	13 b	14 a	15 b	16 d
17 c	18 c	19 d	20 a				

Exercise 3.2 *page 21*

1 c	2 d	3 a	4 b	5 a	6 d	7 b	8 b
9 c	10 b	11 b	12 a	13 a	14 d	15 d	16 b
17 a	18 c	19 a	20 c	21 d	22 b	23 a	24 c
25 a	26 d	27 c	28 b	29 a	30 b		

Exercise 3.3   *page 23*

1 b	2 c	3 b	4 b	5 c	6 a	7 c	8 b
9 a	10 a	11 a	12 c	13 a	14 a	15 b	16 b
17 a	18 a	19 c	20 b	21 a	22 c	23 b	24 c
25 b							

Exercise 3.4   *page 24*

| 1 a | 2 c | 3 a | 4 b | 5 b | 6 b | 7 c | 8 b |
| 9 a | 10 b | | | | | | |

Exercise 3.5   *page 24*

1 b	2 a	3 b	4 d	5 a	6 b	7 b	8 c
9 d	10 a	11 d	12 c	13 b	14 a	15 a	16 c
17 b	18 a	19 a	20 c				

Exercise 3.6   *page 25*

1 a	2 c	3 b	4 a	5 a	6 b	7 c	8 b
9 b	10 a	11 b	12 c	13 b	14 a	15 c	16 a
17 b	18 a	19 b	20 b				

Exercise 3.7   *page 25*

| 1 b | 2 a | 3 b | 4 c | 5 a | 6 b | 7 c | 8 a |
| 9 a | 10 b | | | | | | |

Exercise 3.8   *page 26*

1 9	2 42, 18	3 £3.65	4 12 s	5 33, 63
6 2nd July, 29th July		7 883, 27	8 17	
9 Peter by 4 points		10 via Widnes and Warrington by 6 km		

Exercise 3.9   *page 27*

3 and **8** are not magic squares

Exercise 3.10   *page 27*

```
1  2 7 6        2   6 12  3      3   9 5  4       4   7 12  5
   9 5 1            4  7 10          1 6 11           6  8 10
   4 3 8           11  2  8          8 7  3          11  4  9

5  14 11  7  2   6  10  5 17  6   7   6 12 11  9   8  10  5  8 11
    1  8 12 13       8 15  3 12       17  3  4 14       3 16 13  2
    4  5  9 16       7 16  4 11        5 15 16  2      15  4  1 14
   15 10  6  3      13  2 14  9       10  8  7 13       6  9 12  7

9   3 22  1 20 19              10    8 25 18 15  4
   24  8 15 16  2                    7 11 22  9 21
   17 21 13  5  9                   26 12 14 16  2
   14 10 11 18 12                    5 19  6 17 23
    7  4 25  6 23                   24  3 10 13 20
```

Exercise 3.11   *page 28*

1 34	2 34	3 34	4 36	5 34	6 32	7 34	8 24
9 44	10 34	11 26	12 34	13 42	14 40	15 34	16 34
17 34	18 28	19 34	20 34				

Book 1 Unit 4

| AT 4/3 (i) | Pupils extract and interpret information presented in simple tables and lists. |
| AT 3/3 (ii) | Pupils use non-standard units and standard metric units of length, capacity, mass and time, in a range of contexts. |

Exercise 4.1 *page 29*

1	**a** 9	**b** 22	**c** 5 boys, 4 girls		**d** 90	
2	**a** 1	**b** 1	**c** 3	**d** 1	**e** Tanya	**f** 11
3	**a** 1	**b** Peter	**c** William	**d** 5	**e** 2	**f** 10
4	**a** 1	**b** Sally	**c** 11	**d** 50 p	**e** Martha	**f** £1.39
5	**a** 3		**b** platform 9		**c** 14	
	d 10		**e** platform 8		**f** 41	
6	**a** 6		**b** class 2		**c** 40	
	d 40		**e** Wednesday		**f** class 5 (50)	
7	**a** 50		**b** Saturday		**c** Friday	
	d 65		**e** 110		**f** 30	
8	**a** 25		**b** waiting room bar		**c** 70	
	d 80		**e** waiting room bar		**f** egg	
9	**a** 10		**b** Monday		**c** Sunday	
	d Tuesday		**e** 230		**f** 400	
10	**a** 2	**b** 6	**c** 2	**d** 9	**e** 19	**f** black
11	**a** Shona		**b** Theo		**c** 8	
	d 17		**e** 19		**f** Theo (37)	

Exercise 4.3 *page 34*

1 15	**2** 19	**3** 23	**4** 29	**5** 34	**6** 40	**7** 44
8 51	**9** 58	**10** 63	**11** 70	**12** 78	**13** 87	**14** 91
15 103	**16** 1992	**17** 1988	**18** 1986	**19** 1982	**20** 1971	**21** 1968
22 1963	**23** 1957	**24** 1950	**25** 1946	**26** 1932	**27** 1929	**28** 1920
29 1908	**30** 1904					

Exercise 4.4 *page 34*

1 27	**2** 46	**3** 36	**4** 28	**5** 37
6 9	**7** 28	**8** 33	**9** 14	**10** 27
11 29th Jan	**12** 27th Jan	**13** 21st Mar	**14** 17th Jan	**15** 16th May
16 28th Jan	**17** 13th Jan	**18** 14th Jan	**19** 4th July	**20** 5th Aug
21 3rd Feb	**22** 4th Feb	**23** 2nd Apr	**24** 5th Feb	**25** 9th Feb

Exercise 4.5 *page 35*

1 75	**2** 84	**3** 87	**4** 79	**5** 92	**6** 97	**7** 88	**8** 101
9 98	**10** 109	**11** 120	**12** 115	**13** 130	**14** 134	**15** 123	**16** 129
17 80	**18** 55	**19** 54	**20** 65				

Exercise 4.6 *page 35*

1 11.30 h	**2** 10.15 h	**3** 09.20 h	**4** 07.25 h	**5** 08.45 h
6 05.40 h	**7** 02.10 h	**8** 03.50 h	**9** 01.55 h	**10** 04.00 h
11 06.05 h	**12** 15.30 h	**13** 14.15 h	**14** 18.10 h	**15** 16.25 h
16 19.45 h	**17** 17.35 h	**18** 13.40 h	**19** 20.20 h	**20** 21.55 h
21 19.00 h	**22** 18.25 h	**23** 15.05 h	**24** 21.50 h	**25** 20.00 h
26 22.20 h	**27** 23.15 h	**28** 22.55 h	**29** 23.35 h	**30** 24.00 h

Exercise 4.7 *page 36*

1 11.15 a.m.	**2** 10.20 a.m.	**3** 9.10 a.m.	**4** 8.30 a.m.
5 4.25 a.m.	**6** 2.45 a.m.	**7** 3.40 a.m.	**8** 1.50 a.m.
9 5.35 a.m.	**10** 7.00 a.m.	**11** 12.30 a.m.	**12** 2.30 p.m.
13 4.10 p.m.	**14** 5.15 p.m.	**15** 6.45 p.m.	**16** 1.50 p.m.
17 3.40 p.m.	**18** 4.35 p.m.	**19** 7.05 p.m.	**20** 8.15 p.m.

21 9.20 p.m.	**22** 11.00 p.m.	**23** 10.30 p.m.	**24** 10.05 p.m.
25 11.25 p.m.	**26** 11.50 p.m.	**27** 8.55 p.m.	**28** 9.45 p.m.
29 7.40 p.m.	**30** 6.05 p.m.		

Exercise 4.8 *page 36*

1 35 min	**2** 1 h 15 min	**3** 2 h 30 min	**4** 2 h 40 min
5 25 min	**6** 3 h 35 min	**7** 5 h 25 min	**8** 1 h 15 min
9 40 min	**10** 25 min	**11** 1 h 40 min	**12** 2 h 15 min
13 1 h 5 min	**14** 45 min	**15** 4 h 5 min	**16** 20 min
17 1 h 35 min	**18** 25 min		

19 1 h 5 min, 1 h 30 min, 2 h, 2 h 20 min, 2 h 35 min
20 35 min, 50 min, 1 h 10 min, 1 h 30 min, 2 h 15 min
21 a 8.10 a.m., 6.05 p.m., 8.50 a.m., 6.30 p.m.
　　b 08.15 h, 20 min, 25 min, 15.50 h, 20 min
　　c 11.05 h, 20 min, 5 min, 15.55 h, 4 h 25 min
22 a 9.20 a.m., 6.30 p.m., 8.25 a.m., 5.30 p.m.
　　b 13.50 h, 25 min, 15 min, 17.20 h, 50 min
　　c 12.50 h, 30 min, 40 min, 18.30 h, 4 h 20 min

Book 1　Unit 5

AT 2/3 (iv)　Pupils use mental recall of the 2, 5 and 10 multiplication tables, and others up to 5 × 5, in solving whole-number problems involving multiplication and division, including those that give rise to remainders. Pupils use calculator methods where numbers include several digits.

Exercise 5.1 *page 38*

1 c	**2** a	**3** c	**4** b	**5** c
6 c	**7** a	**8** c	**9** b	**10** a

Exercise 5.2 *page 38*

1 a	**2** a	**3** b	**4** a	**5** c
6 a	**7** b	**8** a	**9** b	**10** a

Exercise 5.3 *page 38*

1 675	**2** 1462	**3** 1224	**4** 588	**5** 4840
6 2037	**7** 780	**8** 1140	**9** 3520	**10** 1958
11 1855	**12** 1008	**13** 765	**14** 1300	**15** 1350
16 2322	**17** 4108	**18** 1428	**19** 2225	**20** 5445

Exercise 5.4 *page 39*

1 4650	**2** 3600	**3** 4752	**4** 960	**5** 8250 ml
6 19 125 g	**7** 16 425	**8** 50 625	**9** £4725	**10** 12 375

Exercise 5.5 *page 40*

1 a	**2** b	**3** a	**4** a	**5** c
6 a	**7** b	**8** c	**9** b	**10** b

Exercise 5.6 *page 40*

1 b	**2** c	**3** b	**4** b	**5** a
6 b	**7** b	**8** a	**9** a	**10** a

Exercise 5.7 *page 41*

1 c	**2** b	**3** a	**4** a	**5** c
6 b	**7** a	**8** c	**9** c	**10** b

Exercise 5.8 *page 41*

1 18 cars, 3 seats　　　　　　　　**2** 53 trays, 5 switches left over
3 1985 trays, 5 apples left over　　**4** £16 640
5 a £53　　　　　　**b** £2756

6	**a**	2123	**b**	7 full books, 29 tickets		
7	**a**	342	**b**	10 full boxes, 17 cans		
8	**a**	£125	**b**	£8500		
9	**a**	£9.00	**b**	212		
10	**a**	5 days	**b**	10 days	**c**	16 days, 40 ml left over
11		£2.66				
12	**a**	£2.10	**b**	£2.66	**c**	£2.66

Book 1 Unit 6

AT 3/4 (i)   Pupils make 3-D mathematical models by linking given faces or edges.

Exercise 6.1 *page 44*   The following are nets for a cube: **2, 3, 4, 5, 6, 8, 9**

Exercise 6.2 *page 45*   **1** 2 cm cubes

Exercise 6.3 *page 46*   **2** 4   **3** 4   **4** 6

Exercise 6.4 *page 46*   **2** 8   **3** 6   **4** 12

Exercise 6.5 *page 47*   **2** 5   **3** 6   **4** 9

Book 1 Unit 7

AT 2/4 (vi)   Pupils explore and describe number patterns, and relationships including multiple, factor and square.

Exercise 7.1 *page 49*
1 a Leanne, William, Jason   **b** Molly, Anya, Pritesh
2 a 6, 8, 10, 12, 14   **b** 18, 20, 22, 24, 26
    c 34, 36, 38, 40, 42   **d** 90, 92, 94, 96, 98
    e 102, 104, 106, 108, 110
3 a 7, 9, 11, 13, 15   **b** 15, 17, 19, 21, 23
    c 33, 35, 37, 39, 41   **d** 71, 73, 75, 77, 79
    e 119, 121, 123, 125, 127

Exercise 7.2 *page 49*
1 a C   **b** A   **c** B
2 a R   **b** R   **c** R, S   **d** R, T   **e** N
    f R   **g** N   **h** S   **i** R, T   **j** R, S, T
4 a 9   **b** 16   **c** 25   **d** 100   **e** 10 000
5 a 4   **b** 9   **c** 16   **d** 25   **e** 36   **f** square

Exercise 7.3 *page 50*   **1** C   **2** 2, 3, 5, 7, 11, 13, 17, 19, 23, 29   **3 a, c, f, h, i, l**

Exercise 7.4 *page 50*
1 22 m, 26 m
2 a 10, 12, 14, 16, 18   **b** 15, 18, 21, 24, 27   **c** 60, 72, 84, 96, 108
    d 30, 25, 20, 15, 10   **e** 42, 36, 30, 24, 18   **f** 28, 21, 14, 7, 0
    g 28, 33, 38, 43, 48   **h** 29, 35, 41, 47, 53   **i** 24, 20, 16, 12, 8
    j 58, 50, 42, 34, 26

3 27

4 a 16, 32, 64   **b** 256, 1024, 4096   **c** 2000, 20 000, 200 000

   d 4, 2, 1   **e** 9, 3, 1   **f** 25, 5, 1

5 a 9   **b** 10   **c** 14   **d** 85   **e** 64   **f** 55

   g 3   **h** 6   **i** 50   **j** 15   **k** 16   **l** 9

Exercise 7.5   *page 51*

1 2, 4, 6, 8   **2** 5, 10, 15, 20   **3** 3, 6, 9, 12

4 6, 12, 18, 24   **5** 10, 20, 30, 40   **6** 7, 14, 21, 28

7 9, 18, 27, 36   **8** 11, 22, 33, 44   **9** 12, 24, 36, 48

10 20, 40, 60, 80   **11** 50, 100, 150, 200   **12** 40, 80, 120, 160

13 60, 120, 180, 240   **14** 25, 50, 75, 100   **15** 15, 30, 45, 60

Exercise 7.6   *page 51*

1 13   **2** 40   **3** 62   **4** 38   **5** 74

6 112   **7** 34   **8** 150   **9** 70   **10** 185

Exercise 7.7   *page 51*

1 12   **2** 30   **3** 90   **4** 20   **5** 40

6 15   **7** 8   **8** 12   **9** 6   **10** 10

11 12   **12** 30   **13** 12   **14** 24   **15** 18

16 36   **17** 45   **18** 30   **19** 24   **20** 60

21 30   **22** 36   **23** 12   **24** 20   **25** 30

Exercise 7.8   *page 52*

1 1, 2, 3, 6, 9, 18   **2** 1, 2, 4, 5, 10, 20   **3** 1, 2, 3, 4, 6, 12

4 1, 2, 5, 10   **5** 1, 2, 4, 8   **6** 1, 2, 7, 14

7 1, 2, 11, 22   **8** 1, 3, 5, 15   **9** 1, 3, 7, 21

10 1, 3, 9, 27   **11** 1, 5, 7, 35   **12** 1, 2, 13, 26

13 1, 2, 4, 7, 14, 28   **14** 1, 2, 4, 8, 16, 32   **15** 1, 2, 3, 5, 6, 10, 15, 30

16 1, 2, 4, 5, 8, 10, 20, 40   **17** 1, 2, 3, 4, 6, 9, 12, 18, 36

18 1, 3, 9   **19** 1, 5, 25   **20** 1, 2, 4, 8, 16

Exercise 7.9   *page 52*

1 8   **2** 12   **3** 9   **4** 6   **5** 12

6 8   **7** 6   **8** 12   **9** 6   **10** 8

11 9   **12** 16   **13** 15   **14** 20   **15** 16

16 18   **17** 14   **18** 15   **19** 24   **20** 21

21 6   **22** 9   **23** 8   **24** 18   **25** 15

Exercise 7.10   *page 52*

1 $2 \times 3 \times 5$ **2** $2 \times 3 \times 11$ **3** $2 \times 5 \times 7$

4 $2 \times 3 \times 13$ **5** $2 \times 5 \times 11$ **6** $2 \times 5 \times 13$

7 $2 \times 7 \times 11$ **8** $2 \times 3 \times 5 \times 7$ **9** $2 \times 2 \times 3 \times 7$

10 $2 \times 2 \times 5 \times 7$ **11** $2 \times 2 \times 3 \times 11$ **12** $2 \times 2 \times 2 \times 11$

13 $2 \times 2 \times 2 \times 13$ **14** $2 \times 2 \times 2 \times 7$ **15** $2 \times 2 \times 2 \times 5$

16 $2 \times 2 \times 2 \times 3 \times 5$ **17** $2 \times 2 \times 2 \times 3 \times 3$ **18** $2 \times 2 \times 2 \times 3 \times 7$

19 $2 \times 2 \times 2 \times 2 \times 5$ **20** $2 \times 2 \times 2 \times 2 \times 3$ **21** $2 \times 2 \times 2 \times 2 \times 7$

22 $2 \times 2 \times 3 \times 3 \times 5$ **23** $2 \times 2 \times 3 \times 3 \times 3$ **24** $2 \times 3 \times 3 \times 3 \times 3$

Exercise 7.11   *page 53*

1 b   **2** b   **3** a   **4** b   **5** c

6 c   **7** a   **8** c   **9** b   **10** c

Exercise 7.12 *page 53*

1
$$3 \leftarrow 5 \quad 11$$
$$4 \quad 7 \leftarrow 9$$
$$6 \leftarrow 8 \leftarrow 10$$

2
$$2 \leftarrow 6 \leftarrow 10$$
$$12 \quad 18 \rightarrow 14$$
$$16 \leftarrow 20 \leftarrow 24$$

3
$$16 \quad 13 \leftarrow 9$$
$$12 \quad 0 \quad 5$$
$$8 \leftarrow 4 \quad 1$$

4
$$24 \quad 6 \leftarrow 0$$
$$18 \leftarrow 12 \quad 10$$
$$28 \leftarrow 22 \leftarrow 16$$

5
$$3 \quad 7 \leftarrow 14$$
$$6 \quad 48 \quad 28$$
$$12 \leftarrow 24 \quad 56$$

6
$$9 \rightarrow 3 \rightarrow 1$$
$$27 \quad 54 \quad 2$$
$$81 \quad 18 \rightarrow 6$$

7
$$64 \leftarrow 32 \quad 48$$
$$8 \rightarrow 16 \quad 24$$
$$4 \quad 6 \rightarrow 12$$

8
$$64 \leftarrow 16 \leftarrow 4$$
$$32 \quad \tfrac{1}{4} \rightarrow 1$$
$$8 \leftarrow 2 \leftarrow \tfrac{1}{2}$$

Exercise 7.13 *page 54*

1 'is a factor of'   **2** 'is a factor of'
3 'is a multiple of'   **4** 'is the square of'
5 'is a multiple of'   **6** 'is a prime factor of'
7 'is a multiple of'   **8** 'is the square of'
9 'is a multiple of'   **10** 'is a prime factor of'

Exercise 7.16 *page 56*

1 $x > 7$ **2** $x > 5$ **3** $y > 9$ **4** $x \geqslant 4$ **5** $x \geqslant 9$
6 $a \geqslant 1$ **7** $b \geqslant 8$ **8** $x < 4$ **9** $p < 6$ **10** $q < 2$
11 $r < 10$ **12** $x \leqslant 4$ **13** $a \leqslant 9$ **14** $b \leqslant 3$ **15** $c \leqslant 12$

Book 1 Unit 8

AT 4/3 (ii)	Pupils construct bar charts and pictograms, where the symbol represents a group of units, to communicate information they have gathered, and they interpret information presented to them in these forms.
AT 4/4 (i)	Pupils collect discrete data and record them using a frequency table.
AT 4/4 (iii)	Pupils group data, where appropriate, in equal class intervals, representing collected data in frequency diagrams and interpreting such diagrams.

Exercise 8.1 *page 58*

1 a 1000   **b** £600   **2 a** 600   **b** £630
3 a 150   **b** £120   **4 a** 200   **b** £2250
5 a 90   **b** 6 h
6 a 4, 8, 5, 7, 3, 1   **b** 15   **c** 27   **d** 50
7 a 6, 11, 15, 4, 3   **b** 25   **c** 10   **d** 50
8 a 21   **b** 30   **9 a** 38   **b** 50
15 a 80   **b** £160   **16 a** 150   **b** £55–50

Exercise 8.3 *page 66*

1 330   **2 a** 120   **b** £1800   **3 a** 200   **b** £600

Exercise 8.4   *page 69*

1	1–2	3–4	5–6	7–8	9–10	11–12	13–14	15–16	17–18	19–20
	7	9	10	11	7	9	15	16	9	7

2	1–5	6–10	11–15	16–20
	22	22	33	23

5	mark	group 1	group 2
	1–10	0	0
	11–20	5	1
	21–30	5	4
	31–40	23	7
	41–50	9	4
	51–60	12	13
	61–70	11	12
	71–80	5	22
	81–90	8	13
	91–100	2	4

Book 1 Unit 9

AT 2/4 (ii)	In solving number problems, pupils use a range of mental and writtethods of computation with the four operations, including mental recall of multiplication facts up to 10×10.
AT 2/4 (iv)	In solving problems with or without a calculator, pupils check the reasonableness of their resuls by reference to their knowledge of the context or to the size of the numbers.
AT 2/5 (vi)	Pupils check their solutions by applying inverse operations or estimating using approximations.
Revision of:	
AT 2/3 (iii)	Pupils use mental recall of addition and subtraction facts to 20 in solving problems involving larger numbers.
AT 2/3 (v)	Pupils have begun to develop mental strategies, and use them to find methods for adding and subtracting numbers with at least two digits.

Exercise 9.1   *page 71*

1 b	2 b	3 a	4 a	5 c
6 b	7 a	8 a	9 c	10 b

Exercise 9.2   *page 71*

1 c	2 b	3 c	4 a	5 a
6 c	7 a	8 b	9 a	10 a
11 a	12 b	13 b	14 c	15 a

Exercise 9.3   *page 72*

1 720	2 650	3 840	4 1120	5 1920	6 4050
7 8640	8 8470	9 8520	10 7800	11 2700	12 4800
13 8000	14 35 000	15 5600	16 9600	17 22 800	18 29 600
19 92 800	20 68 000	21 72 800	22 84 000	23 72 000	24 96 000

Exercise 9.4   *page 72*

1 585	2 384	3 576	4 646	5 855
6 406	7 768	8 1092	9 1848	10 1625
11 b	12 b	13 a	14 a	15 c
16 b	17 a	18 b	19 b	20 c

Exercise 9.5 *page 72*

1 120, 108	**2** 270, 306	**3** 180, 184	**4** 640, 608
5 500, 624	**6** 420, 413	**7** 540, 513	**8** 300, 350
9 2000, 2322	**10** 7000, 6624	**11** 3200, 3034	**12** 6000, 7104
13 20 000, 18 972	**14** 48 000, 49 973	**15** 35 000, 32 040	**16** 48 000, 41 615
17 120 000, 112 914	**18** 4200, 4389	**19** 120 000, 155 848	
20 90 000, 79 513	**21** 720 000, 706 936	**22** 120 000, 106 088	
23 80 000, 94 530	**24** 480 000, 447 513	**25** 21 600 000, 18 428 340	

Exercise 9.6 *page 73*

1 300, 315	**2** 360, 340	**3** 420, 390	**4** 640, 632
5 2100, 1944	**6** 3200, 3154	**7** 1200, 1188	**8** 800, 663
9 1500, 1395	**10** 28 000, 29 160	**11** 16 000, 13 296	**12** 18 000, 18 150
13 81 000, 82 432	**14** 42 000, 40 560	**15** 16 000, 13 861	**16** 80 000, 98 982
17 140 000, 122 607	**18** 120 000, 95 206	**19** 360 000, 393 736	
20 60 000, 76 936	**21** 250 000, 227 205	**22** 300 000, 326 106	
23 900 000, 901 530	**24** 100 000, 110 889	**25** 250 000, 247 050	

Exercise 9.7 *page 73*

1 72 cm	**2** 96 km, 128 km	**3** 948 m	**4** 90 m
5 84	**6** 104	**7** 120	**8** 105, 630
9 390 t	**10** 325 m		

Exercise 9.8 *page 74*

1 b	**2** a	**3** d	**4** a	**5** c	**6** d
7 b	**8** b	**9** c	**10** a	**11** d	**12** c

Exercise 9.9 *page 75*

1 c	**2** d	**3** b	**4** d	**5** b	**6** a
7 a	**8** b	**9** a	**10** c	**11** b	**12** b
13 a	**14** c	**15** b			

Exercise 9.10 *page 75*

1 15	**2** 13	**3** 12	**4** 24	**5** 23	**6** 32
7 31	**8** 30	**9** 45	**10** 42	**11** 54	**12** 63
13 a	**14** c	**15** b	**16** b	**17** c	**18** a
19 c	**20** b	**21** a	**22** b	**23** a	**24** c
25 13 r 3	**26** 15 r 10	**27** 14 r 10	**28** 13 r 9	**29** 11 r 8	**30** 12 r 6

Exercise 9.11 *page 76*

1 5, 6	**2** 5, 5	**3** 10, 8	**4** 70, 55	**5** 10, 11	**6** 8, 9
7 45, 39	**8** 23, 22	**9** 40, 43	**10** 10, 9	**11** 4, 5	
12 25, 22.42 (22 r 10)		**13** 10, 11.53 (11 r 20)		**14** 20, 19.15 (19 r 5)	
15 23, 23.46 (23 r 17)		**16** 13, 13		**17** 10, 9.29 (9 r 12)	
18 45, 46.84 (46 r 16)		**19** 15, 15.74 (15 r 31)		**20** 13, 16.42 (16 r 11)	

Exercise 9.12 *page 76*

1 30, 27.15 (27 r 5)	**2** 20, 21.57 (21 r 21)	**3** 15, 14.38 (14 r 8)
4 30, 19.92 (19 r 12)	**5** 35, 32.77 (32 r 17)	**6** 20, 17.79 (17 r 26)
7 15, 15.44 (15 r 17)	**8** 45, 49.53 (49 r 10)	**9** 80, 63.54 (63 r 7)
10 5, 4.71 (4 r 15)	**11** 20, 21.70 (21 r 32)	**12** 25, 26.58 (26 r 21)
13 10, 9.75 (9 r 76)	**14** 3, 3.01 (3 r 2)	**15** 2, 2.23 (2 r 81)
16 2, 2.44 (2 r 170)	**17** 60, 42.64 (42 r 9)	**18** 35, 43.4 (43 r 6)
19 23, 26.31 (26 r 11)	**20** 5, 4.93 (4 r 52)	

Exercise 9.13 *page 77*

1 155 ml	**2** 66	**3** 19 weeks	**4** 13	**5** 64
6 19 cm	**7** 119 km	**8** 45 kg	**9** 35 g	**10** 48
11 78	**12** 14 km	**13** 5 cm	**14** 16, 40 ml	**15** 16, 12 t

Exercise 9.14   *page 78*

a

8	6		6	2		2
	5	2		3	7	5
2		4	6		5	
5	3		9	4		4
4	2	5		3	3	6
		8	2		4	
6	3	7		5	5	6

b

3	4		5	3		9
	7	6		6	5	2
4		6	8		5	
4	5		3	9		8
2	5	3		3	4	7
		8	7		5	
4	2	9		5	8	4

c

7	2		8	4		3
	7	5		8	5	2
1		9	8		6	
9	2		8	7		6
8	8	2		6	2	0
		9	0		3	
9	3	6		7	6	8

d

1	9		3	8		8
	9	7		4	7	5
8		6	9		8	
8	9		5	9		9
2	6	9		1	9	2
		4	5		7	
1	9	2		1	2	3

e

1	6		1	5		2
	4	9		3	6	5
1		1	4		1	
2	1		1	1		6
1	2	1		1	1	0
		1	0		0	
1	1	2		1	0	0

Exercise 9.15   *page 79*

1 879	**2** 726	**3** 984	**4** 865	**5** 926	**6** 751
7 a	**8** d	**9** c	**10** a	**11** b	**12** c
13 c	**14** d	**15** a	**16** b	**17** d	**18** c
19 423	**20** 245	**21** 154	**22** 51	**23** 324	**24** 276
25 b	**26** c	**27** d	**28** b	**29** a	**30** a
31 c	**32** b				

33 $312 + 452 + 323$ **34** $534 + 313 + 232$
35 $331 + 243 + 612$ **36** $835 + 320 + 143$ **37** $513 + 342 + 402$
38 $8985 - 6362$ **39** $8878 - 3632$ **40** $9565 - 2402$
41 $8928 - 5520$ **42** $3969 - 1259$ **43** $9967 - 3125$
44 $4897 - 4520$

Exercise 9.16   *page 80*

1 1424	**2** 1265	**3** 1206	**4** 1920	**5** 1215	**6** 1421
7 2580	**8** 3150	**9** c	**10** a	**11** b	**12** d
13 c	**14** b	**15** 231	**16** 216	**17** 131	**18** 247
19 206	**20** 130	**21** 31	**22** 22	**23** a	**24** b
25 d	**26** c	**27** a	**28** c	**29** 48×4	**30** 32×8

31 132×3 **32** 218×4 **33** 134×5 **34** $375 \div 5$ **35** $612 \div 9$
36 $625 \div 5$ **37** $726 \div 3$ **38** $832 \div 4$ **39** $720 \div 6$ **40** $810 \div 9$

Exercise 9.17   *page 80*

1 a 108 cm   **b** 12 cm   **c** 84 cm
2 a 982 m   **b** 8838 m
3 65 g   **4** 300 g
5 a 625 km   **b** 434 km   **c** 217 km   **d** 842 km
6 448 m, 319 m   **7** 9570, 3190, 290   **8** 470 m, 94 m   **9** 8 g

Book 2   Unit 1

AT 2/3 (ii)	Pupils have begun to use deciman notation in contexts such as money, temperature and calculator displays.
AT 2/4 (iii)	Pupils add and subtract decimals to two places.
AT 2/5 (i)	Pupils use their understanding of place value to multiply and divide whole numbers and decimals by 10, 100 and 1000.

Exercise 1.1 *page 1*

1 0.5	**2** 0.2	**3** 0.07	**4** 0.09	**5** 0.02
6 0.05	**7** 0.06	**8** 0.4	**9** 0.1	**10** 0.6
11 0.8	**12** 0.2	**13** 0.05	**14** 0.07	**15** 0.01
16 0.006	**17** 0.005	**18** 0.002	**19** 0.03	**20** 0.04
21 0.006	**22** 0.007	**23** 0.004	**24** 0.006	**25** 0.003

Exercise 1.2 *page 1*

1 5, 5.02, 5.2, 5.22   **2** 4, 4.03, 4.3, 4.33
3 7, 7.004, 7.04, 7.044, 7.4, 7.44   **4** 8, 8.005, 8.05, 8.055, 8.5, 8.55
5 3, 3.001, 3.01, 3.011, 3.1, 3.11   **6** 0.53, 5.03, 5.3, 5.33
7 0.72, 7.02, 7.2, 7.22   **8** 0.65, 6.05, 6.5, 6.55
9 0.324, 3.024, 3.204, 3.24, 32.4   **10** 0.561, 5.061, 5.601, 5.61, 56.1
11 0.483, 4.083, 4.803, 4.83, 48.03, 48.3
12 0.275, 2.075, 2.705, 2.75, 27.05, 27.5

Exercise 1.3 *page 1*

1 3.56, 65.3	**2** 1.48, 84.1	**3** 2.39, 93.2	**4** 4.57, 75.4
5 0.25, 52.0	**6** 0.67, 76.0	**7** 1.235, 532.1	**8** 4.567, 765.4
9 3.489, 984.3	**10** 1.356, 653.1	**11** 2.478, 874.2	**12** 0.235, 532.0
13 0.178, 871.0	**14** 0.034, 430.0	**15** 0.079, 970.0	

Exercise 1.4 *page 2*

1 32.5	**2** 53.6	**3** 18.4	**4** 40.5	**5** 20.8	**6** 54
7 82	**8** 91	**9** 2.6	**10** 5.7	**11** 8.9	**12** 3
13 9	**14** 1	**15** 0.3	**16** 0.7	**17** 4.25	**18** 6.41
19 1.18	**20** 4.02	**21** 1.05	**22** 0.04	**23** 0.09	**24** 0.54
25 0.17	**26** 45.3	**27** 62.7	**28** 12.1	**29** 50.8	**30** 90.6
31 6.4	**32** 3.8	**33** 0.5	**34** 0.2	**35** 36	**36** 92
37 55	**38** 4	**39** 9	**40** 30	**41** 80	**42** 10
43 527	**44** 394	**45** 122	**46** 203	**47** 606	**48** 520
49 390	**50** 110				

Exercise 1.5 *page 2*

1 0.56	**2** 0.32	**3** 0.97	**4** 0.435	**5** 0.158
6 0.216	**7** 0.309	**8** 0.5	**9** 0.8	**10** 0.2
11 2.54	**12** 6.71	**13** 9.57	**14** 5.06	**15** 3.2
16 7.5	**17** 9.9	**18** 0.019	**19** 0.083	**20** 0.055
21 0.03	**22** 0.07	**23** 0.01	**24** 0.005	**25** 0.002

26 0.352	**27** 0.816	**28** 0.405	**29** 0.201	**30** 0.37
31 0.62	**32** 0.5	**33** 1.25	**34** 2.36	**35** 0.0534
36 0.0995	**37** 0.0474	**38** 0.0108	**39** 0.058	**40** 0.036
41 0.015	**42** 0.0027	**43** 0.0061	**44** 0.0032	**45** 0.0005
46 0.0008	**47** 0.0004	**48** 0.008	**49** 0.003	**50** 0.001

Exercise 1.6 *page 2*

1, 2 and **3** $2.6 \times 10 = 26$ **4, 5** and **6** $3.25 \times 10 = 32.5$
7, 8 and **9** $5.42 \times 100 = 542$ **10, 11** and **12** $4.8 \times 100 = 480$
13, 14 and **15** $18.6 \div 10 = 1.86$ **16, 17** and **18** $3.41 \div 10 = 0.341$
19 and **20** $61.5 \div 100 = 0.615$

Exercise 1.7 *page 3*

1 34 560	**2** 2450	**3** 13 000	**4** 130
5 1600	**6** 5900	**7** 6300	**8** 3660
9 56	**10** 1	**11** 100	**12** 123 000
13 123	**14** 12 300	**15** 1230	**16** 12.3
17 683 340	**18** 1.23	**19** 6833.4	**20** 6 833 400
21 68 334 000	**22** 683.34	**23** 0.001	**24** 45 990
25 500 005	**26** 0.678	**27** 0.0678	**28** 0.006 78
29 0.000 678	**30** 0.000 067 8	**31** 4	**32** 0.4
33 0.04	**34** 0.004	**35** 0.0004	**36** 0.000 04
37 0.000 004	**38** 55.555	**39** 5.5555	**40** 0.555 55
41 0.055 555	**42** 0.005 555 5	**43** 0.000 555 55	**44** 0.034 67
45 0.060 04	**46** 12.789	**47** 0.045 01	**48** 0.007
49 0.000 000 7	**50** 1		

Exercise 1.8 *page 3*

1 20×1000	**2** 2×1000
3 0.2×1000	**4** 0.02×1000
5 0.002×1000	**6** 0.0002×1000
7 $0.000 02 \times 1000$	**8** $0.000 002 \times 1000$
9 $0.000 000 2 \times 1000$	**10** 0.756×1000
11 2.908×1000	**12** $0.034 26 \times 1000$
13 0.0005×1000	**14** 5×1000
15 0.0679×1000	**16** 8.9045×1000
17 25×1000	**18** $0.000 855 \times 1000$
19 0.001×1000	**20** $0.000 017 \times 1000$
21 $50 000 000 \div 1000$	**22** $5 000 000 \div 1000$
23 $500 000 \div 1000$	**24** $50 000 \div 1000$
25 $5000 \div 1000$	**26** $500 \div 1000$
27 $50 \div 1000$	**28** $5 \div 1000$
29 $0.5 \div 1000$	**30** $23 000 \div 1000$
31 $230 \div 1000$	**32** $4007 \div 1000$
33 $12 400 \div 1000$	**34** $1240 \div 1000$
35 $124 000 \div 1000$	**36** $1 \div 1000$
37 $0.1 \div 1000$	**38** $1 000 000 \div 1000$
39 $1000 \div 1000$	**40** $3142 \div 1000$

Exercise 1.9 *page 4*

1 b	**2** a	**3** d	**4** b	**5** c
6 b	**7** a	**8** a	**9** d	**10** c

Exercise 1.10 *page 4*

1 b	**2** a	**3** a	**4** c	**5** b	**6** a
7 a	**8** c	**9** b	**10** a	**11** b	**12** b
13 a	**14** b	**15** a	**16** b	**17** c	**18** c

Exercise 1.11 *page 5*

1 a	2 b	3 b	4 d	5 c
6 d	7 a	8 a	9 c	10 b
11 d	12 a	13 c	14 b	15 d
16 a	17 c	18 c	19 d	20 a

Exercise 1.12 *page 5*

1 b	2 a	3 a	4 c	5 a
6 a	7 b	8 b	9 c	10 c
11 a	12 b	13 c	14 a	15 b

Exercise 1.13 *page 6*

1 b	2 b	3 a	4 c	5 b
6 a	7 a	8 c	9 b	10 a
11 b	12 c	13 a	14 b	15 b
16 a	17 c	18 b	19 a	20 c

Exercise 1.14 *page 6*

1 1 m   2 5 m   3 11 m   4 1.75 kg   5 15 p
6 Yes, two short sides and one long side   7 Yes, 67.8 km

Book 2 Unit 2

AT 3/4 (vii)   Pupils find perimeters of simple shapes, find areas by counting squares, and find volumes by counting cubes.

Exercise 2.1 *page 8*

1 18 cm, 8 cm^2 2 20 cm, 9 cm^2 3 20 cm, 9 cm^2
4 24 cm, 12 cm^2 5 20 cm, 13 cm^2 6 8.8 cm, 5 cm^2
7 11.6 cm, 6 cm^2 8 11.2 cm, 8 cm^2 9 13.6 cm, 8 cm^2
10 14.4 cm, 9 cm^2

Exercise 2.2 *page 9*

1 24 cm, 12 cm^2; 24 cm, 12 cm^2; 16 cm, 7 cm^2
2 20 cm, 9 cm^2; 16 cm, 7 cm^2; 20 cm, 9 cm^2
3 20 cm, 10 cm^2; 20 cm, 9 cm^2; 22 cm, 10 cm^2
4 18 cm, 8 cm^2; 20 cm, 9 cm^2; 18 cm, 9 cm^2
5 24 cm, 11 cm^2; 24 cm, 11 cm^2; 24 cm, 12 cm^2
6 18.8 cm, 9 cm^2; 20 cm, 10 cm^2; 22 cm, 10 cm^2
7 22.8 cm, 11 cm^2; 20 cm, 10 cm^2; 22 cm, 10 cm^2
8 24 cm, 11 cm^2; 26.8 cm, 13 cm^2; 22.8 cm, 11 cm^2
9 20.8 cm, 10 cm^2; 21.6 cm, 10 cm^2; 22.8 cm, 10 cm^2
10 26.4 cm, 10 cm^2; 24 cm, 11 cm^2; 18 cm, 8 cm^2

Exercise 2.3 *page 10*

1 10 cm, 6 cm^2 2 12 cm, 8 cm^2 3 14 cm, 12 cm^2
4 16 cm, 15 cm^2 5 14 cm, 10 cm^2 6 16 cm, 12 cm^2
7 18 cm, 18 cm^2 8 10 cm, 4 cm^2 9 8 cm, 4 cm^2
10 12 cm, 9 cm^2

Exercise 2.4 *page 11*

1 a maximum perimeter 34 cm
   b minimum perimeter 16 cm

2 a maximum perimeter 20 cm
   b minimum perimeter 12 cm

3 a maximum perimeter 26 cm
  b minimum perimeter 14 cm

4, 5 and **6** The maximum area for each length of string would be a circle.
The minimum is with the string doubled up: 8 cm, 4.5 cm, 6 cm.

Exercise 2.5 *page 12*

1 cm²	**2** cm²	**3** m²	**4** m²	**5** km²
6 mm²	**7** mm²	**8** m²	**9** cm²	**10** cm²

Exercise 2.6 *page 13*

1 c   **2** a   **3** a   **4** b   **5** b   **6** b   **7** c

Exercise 2.7 *page 13*

1 a   **2** c   **3** b   **4** a   **5** c   **6** a   **7** a

Exercise 2.8 *page 14*

1 36 cm², 26 cm	**2** 56 cm², 30 cm	**3** 54 cm², 30 cm
4 35 cm², 24 cm	**5** 72 cm², 36 cm	**6** 96 cm², 40 cm
7 1500 mm², 160 mm	**8** 7200 mm², 340 mm	**9** 0.9 m², 4.6 m
10 1.8 m², 5.4 m	**11** 6 cm, 28 cm	**12** 3 cm, 24 cm
13 5 cm, 34 cm	**14** 40 mm, 180 mm	**15** 4 mm, 58 mm
16 9 cm, 28 cm	**17** 7 cm, 26 cm	**18** 12 cm, 38 cm
19 15 m, 38 m	**20** 25 m, 56 m	**21** 2 cm, 12 cm²
22 4 cm, 28 cm²	**23** 6 cm, 60 cm²	**24** 20 mm, 800 mm²
25 5 mm, 75 mm²	**26** 6 cm, 24 cm²	**27** 8 cm, 24 cm²
28 10 cm, 90 cm²	**29** 5 m, 20 m²	**30** 8 m, 40 m²

Exercise 2.9 *page 14*

1 12 cm², 20 cm	**2** 7 cm², 16 cm	**3** 12 cm², 26 cm
4 8 cm², 14 cm	**5** 9 cm², 16 cm	

Exercise 2.10 *page 16*

1 20 cm²	**2** 18 cm²	**3** 16 cm²	**4** 18 cm²
5 30 cm²	**6** 25 cm²	**7** 22 cm²	**8** 45 mm²
9 125 mm²	**10** 1200 mm²	**11** 1200 mm²	**12** 1400 mm²
13 0.3 m²	**14** 0.3 m²	**15** 0.4 m²	**16** 5 m²

Exercise 2.11 *page 17*

1 24   **2** 200   **3** 450   **4** 80   **5** 60

Exercise 2.12 *page 18*

1 cube	**2** cuboid	**3** cylinder	**4** cylinder	**5** sphere
6 triangular prism		**7** cone		
8 triangular prism		**9** cylinder, cone		

Exercise 2.13 *page 20*

1 b   **2** a   **3** b   **4** c   **5** b   **6** a   **7** c   **8** b

Exercise 2.14 *page 22*

1 b	**2** c	**3** a	**4** b	**5** a
6 c	**7** a	**8** a	**9** b	**10** a

Exercise 2.15   *page 23*

1 3 cm	2 2 cm	3 4 cm	4 3 cm	5 8 cm
6 7 cm	7 5 cm	8 4 cm	9 5 cm	10 3 cm
11 6 cm	12 12 cm	13 4 m	14 3 m	15 0.5 m

Exercise 2.16   *page 23*

1 4 *l*	2 6 *l*	3 3 *l*	4 10 *l*	5 12 *l*
6 7.5 *l*	7 4.5 *l*	8 1.5 *l*	9 6.3 *l*	10 2.4 *l*
11 5000 *l*	12 8000 *l*	13 2000 *l*	14 14 000 *l*	15 10 000 *l*
16 2500 *l*	17 4200 *l*	18 6250 *l*	19 1250 *l*	20 8750 *l*
21 0.75 *l*	22 0.45 *l*	23 0.6 *l*	24 0.9 *l*	25 0.065 *l*
26 0.045 *l*	27 0.015 *l*	28 0.02 *l*	29 0.08 *l*	30 0.01 *l*

Exercise 2.17   *page 23*

1 8 *l*	2 12 *l*	3 30 *l*	4 12 *l*	5 45 *l*
6 60 000 *l*	7 12 000 *l*	8 18 000 *l*	9 16 000 *l*	10 30 000 *l*
11 400 *l*	12 300 *l*	13 1200 *l*	14 1500 *l*	15 1800 *l*

Exercise 2.18   *page 24*

1 80 *l*	2 30 *l*, 150	3 96	4 9

Exercise 2.19   *page 24*

1 32 cm^2 2 64 cm^2, 96 cm^2 3 49 cm^2
4 10 cm^2, 36 cm^2 5 18 cm^3 6 36 cm^3
7 a 300 cm^3 b 300 ml   c 0.3 *l*
8 480 km   9 yes
10 a 2 m^3 b 2000 *l*
11 a 0.2 m^3 b 200 *l*   c 8
12 50   13 10   14 30   15 960 cm^2
16 a 16 cm^2, 16 cm   b 19.6 cm^2, 19.6 cm   d 3 cm

Book 2   Unit 3

AT 3/4 (iv)	Pupils identify orders of rotational symmetry.
AT 3/5 (ii)	Pupils identify all the symmetries of 2-D shapes.

Rotation is not specifically mentioned in the Attainment Target but is included in the Programme of Study under Shape, Space and Measures:

3b Pupils should be taught to recognise and visualise the transformations of translation, reflection, rotation, and enlargement, and their combination in two dimensions: understand the notations used to describe them.

Exercise 3.1   *page 28*

1 c	2 d	3 b	4 d	5 c	6 a

Exercise 3.2   *page 29*

1 D 1 line of symmetry, A 1 line of symmetry, I rotational symmetry and 2 lines of symmetry, S rotational symmetry only, Y rotational symmetry and 1 line of symmetry
2 Y see above, A see above, C 1 line of symmetry, H see Example 2, T 1 line of symmetry
3 Z rotational symmetry, E see Example 2, B 1 line of symmetry, R and A see above
4 M 1 line of symmetry, I see above, X rotational symmetry and 4 lines of symmetry, E and R see above
5 K 1 line of symmetry, I see above, N rotational symmetry only, G none
6 W 1line of symmetry, O rotational symmetry and 4 lines of symmetry, L 1 line of symmetry, F no lines of symmetry

Exercise 3.3 *page 30*

	Number of lines of symmetry	Rotational symmetry of order
1	7	7
2	5	5
3	6	6
4	3	3
5	8	8
6	12	12
7	10	10
8	9	9

Exercise 3.4 *page 31*

	Number of lines of symmetry	Rotational symmetry of order
1	2	2
2	0	4
3	2	2
4	1	1
5	4	4
6	2	2
7	2	2
8	0	4
9	4	4
10	3	3
11	0	3
12	1	1

Exercise 3.7 *page 36*   **9** $60°$ **10** $45°$

Book 2 Unit 4

AT 2/4 (v)   Pupils recognise approximate proportions of a whole and use simple fractions and percentages to describe these.

Exercise 4.1 *page 39*

1 $\frac{3}{4}$	**2** $\frac{5}{6}$	**3** $\frac{4}{5}$	**4** $\frac{2}{3}$	**5** $\frac{1}{4}$
6 $\frac{2}{3}$	**7** $\frac{3}{4}$	**8** $\frac{1}{3}$	**9** $\frac{2}{3}$	**10** $\frac{1}{3}$

Exercise 4.2 *page 40*

1 c	**2** b	**3** b	**4** b	**5** c
6 b	**7** a	**8** b	**9** b	**10** c

Exercise 4.3 *page 41*

1 c	**2** b	**3** d	**4** d	**5** a
6 d	**7** b	**8** c	**9** a	**10** a
11 b	**12** b	**13** a	**14** c	**15** b
16 b	**17** b	**18** a	**19** c	**20** a
21 b	**22** a	**23** c	**24** a	**25** a

Exercise 4.5 *page 42*

1 $\frac{2}{6}$	**2** $\frac{6}{8}$	**3** $\frac{4}{8}$	**4** $\frac{6}{15}$	**5** $\frac{4}{20}$	**6** $\frac{12}{32}$	**7** $\frac{5}{30}$	**8** $\frac{25}{40}$
9 $\frac{18}{30}$	**10** $\frac{12}{18}$	**11** $\frac{9}{36}$	**12** $\frac{12}{60}$	**13** $\frac{2}{16}$	**14** $\frac{14}{20}$	**15** $\frac{3}{36}$	**16** $\frac{12}{15}$
17 $\frac{4}{36}$	**18** $\frac{20}{28}$	**19** $\frac{15}{40}$	**20** $\frac{25}{30}$	**21** $\frac{18}{24}$	**22** $\frac{14}{35}$	**23** $\frac{32}{40}$	**24** $\frac{24}{36}$
25 $\frac{15}{60}$	**26** $\frac{2}{3}$	**27** $\frac{5}{6}$	**28** $\frac{3}{5}$	**29** $\frac{7}{12}$	**30** $\frac{4}{5}$	**31** $\frac{8}{9}$	**32** $\frac{1}{8}$
33 $\frac{3}{7}$	**34** $\frac{4}{5}$	**35** $\frac{1}{4}$	**36** $\frac{3}{4}$	**37** $\frac{4}{5}$	**38** $\frac{9}{10}$	**39** $\frac{7}{12}$	**40** $\frac{5}{6}$
41 $\frac{7}{11}$	**42** $\frac{5}{8}$	**43** $\frac{5}{12}$	**44** $\frac{7}{12}$	**45** $\frac{8}{9}$	**46** $\frac{5}{6}$	**47** $\frac{1}{9}$	**48** $\frac{5}{6}$

49 $\frac{4}{9}$ 50 $\frac{3}{4}$ 51 $\frac{1}{2}$ 52 $\frac{3}{4}$ 53 $\frac{3}{8}$ 54 $\frac{5}{12}$ 55 $\frac{4}{15}$ 56 $\frac{1}{4}$

57 $\frac{2}{3}$ 58 $\frac{4}{5}$ 59 $\frac{3}{4}$ 60 $\frac{7}{20}$ 61 $\frac{5}{15}$ 62 $\frac{12}{20}$ 63 $\frac{25}{30}$ 64 $\frac{35}{60}$

65 $\frac{9}{20}$ 66 $\frac{5}{30}$ 67 $\frac{16}{24}$ 68 $\frac{55}{60}$ 69 $\frac{24}{60}$ 70 $\frac{15}{100}$

Exercise 4.6   *page 43*

1 $1\frac{1}{6}$ 2 $1\frac{1}{8}$ 3 $1\frac{2}{3}$ 4 $1\frac{3}{7}$ 5 $1\frac{5}{6}$ 6 $1\frac{4}{5}$ 7 $1\frac{5}{8}$ 8 $1\frac{7}{10}$

9 $1\frac{3}{11}$ 10 $1\frac{5}{12}$ 11 $1\frac{1}{4}$ 12 $1\frac{2}{3}$ 13 $1\frac{3}{5}$ 14 $1\frac{1}{3}$ 15 $1\frac{1}{4}$ 16 $1\frac{2}{3}$

17 $1\frac{3}{5}$ 18 $1\frac{1}{2}$ 19 $1\frac{2}{3}$ 20 $1\frac{2}{3}$ 21 $2\frac{1}{2}$ 22 $2\frac{1}{4}$ 23 $2\frac{2}{3}$ 24 $2\frac{4}{5}$

25 $2\frac{1}{4}$ 26 $2\frac{3}{5}$ 27 $2\frac{1}{2}$ 28 $2\frac{2}{3}$ 29 2 30 3 31 $3\frac{1}{3}$ 32 $3\frac{1}{4}$

33 $3\frac{3}{4}$ 34 $3\frac{1}{2}$ 35 $3\frac{2}{3}$ 36 $4\frac{1}{2}$ 37 $4\frac{2}{3}$ 38 $4\frac{1}{4}$ 39 $5\frac{1}{4}$ 40 $5\frac{1}{2}$

Exercise 4.7   *page 43*

1 $\frac{5}{4}$ 2 $\frac{10}{9}$ 3 $\frac{7}{5}$ 4 $\frac{11}{8}$ 5 $\frac{12}{7}$ 6 $\frac{13}{10}$ 7 $\frac{19}{12}$ 8 $\frac{15}{8}$

9 $\frac{7}{3}$ 10 $\frac{11}{5}$ 11 $\frac{11}{4}$ 12 $\frac{13}{5}$ 13 $\frac{16}{7}$ 14 $\frac{7}{2}$ 15 $\frac{16}{5}$ 16 $\frac{11}{3}$

17 $\frac{17}{4}$ 18 $\frac{23}{5}$ 19 $\frac{16}{3}$ 20 $\frac{27}{5}$ 21 $\frac{29}{5}$ 22 $\frac{23}{4}$ 23 $\frac{13}{2}$ 24 $\frac{19}{3}$

25 $\frac{15}{2}$ 26 $\frac{3}{1}$ 27 $\frac{8}{1}$ 28 $\frac{15}{1}$ 29 $\frac{40}{1}$ 30 $\frac{1}{1}$

Exercise 4.8   *page 44*

1 0.2 2 0.6 3 0.1 4 0.9 5 0.18

6 0.26 7 0.42 8 0.54 9 0.62 10 0.86

11 0.78 12 0.02 13 0.15 14 0.35 15 0.65

16 0.95 17 0.05 18 0.16 19 0.24 20 0.36

21 0.48 22 0.72 23 0.08 24 0.75 25 0.122

26 0.106 27 0.105 28 0.408 29 0.125 30 0.875

Exercise 4.9   *page 44*

1 $\frac{3}{10}$ 2 $\frac{19}{100}$ 3 $\frac{27}{100}$ 4 $\frac{81}{100}$ 5 $\frac{99}{100}$

6 $\frac{3}{100}$ 7 $\frac{7}{100}$ 8 $\frac{1}{100}$ 9 $\frac{123}{1000}$ 10 $\frac{361}{1000}$

11 $\frac{729}{1000}$ 12 $\frac{887}{1000}$ 13 $\frac{13}{1000}$ 14 $\frac{61}{1000}$ 15 $\frac{11}{1000}$

16 $\frac{39}{1000}$ 17 $\frac{87}{1000}$ 18 $\frac{9}{1000}$ 19 $\frac{7}{1000}$ 20 $\frac{1}{1000}$

Exercise 4.10   *page 44*

1 $\frac{4}{5}$ 2 $\frac{9}{20}$ 3 $\frac{11}{20}$ 4 $\frac{17}{20}$ 5 $\frac{7}{50}$ 6 $\frac{11}{50}$

7 $\frac{23}{50}$ 8 $\frac{41}{50}$ 9 $\frac{19}{50}$ 10 $\frac{49}{50}$ 11 $\frac{8}{25}$ 12 $\frac{3}{25}$

13 $\frac{11}{25}$ 14 $\frac{16}{25}$ 15 $\frac{18}{25}$ 16 $\frac{14}{25}$ 17 $\frac{7}{40}$ 18 $\frac{9}{40}$

19 $\frac{19}{40}$ 20 $\frac{11}{40}$ 21 $\frac{3}{40}$ 22 $\frac{1}{250}$ 23 $\frac{3}{250}$ 24 $\frac{2}{125}$

25 $\frac{11}{125}$ 26 $\frac{3}{500}$ 27 $\frac{1}{125}$ 28 $\frac{1}{200}$ 29 $\frac{1}{500}$ 30 $\frac{1}{250}$

Exercise 4.11   *page 45*

1 $\frac{4}{5}$, 0.8 2 $1\frac{2}{5}$, 1.4 3 $\frac{7}{10}$, 0.7 4 $\frac{2}{5}$, 0.4 5 $1\frac{1}{10}$, 1.1

6 $\frac{1}{5}$, 0.2 7 $\frac{1}{5}$, 0.2 8 $\frac{3}{5}$, 0.6 9 $\frac{1}{5}$, 0.2 10 $\frac{3}{10}$, 0.3

11 c 12 b 13 b 14 c 15 c 16 a 17 b 18 c

19 a 20 b 21 a 22 c 23 b 24 a 25 a 26 c

Exercise 4.12   *page 46*

1 $\frac{63}{100}$, 0.63 2 $\frac{29}{100}$, 0.29 3 $\frac{13}{100}$, 0.13 4 $\frac{43}{100}$, 0.43 5 $\frac{77}{100}$, 0.77

6 $\frac{9}{100}$, 0.09 7 $\frac{11}{50}$, 0.22 8 $\frac{23}{50}$, 0.46 9 $\frac{41}{50}$, 0.82 10 $\frac{7}{50}$, 0.14

11 $\frac{17}{50}$, 0.34 12 $\frac{49}{50}$, 0.98 13 $\frac{29}{50}$, 0.58 14 $\frac{11}{20}$, 0.55 15 $\frac{17}{20}$, 0.85

16 $\frac{3}{20}$, 0.15 17 $\frac{1}{20}$, 0.05 18 $\frac{12}{25}$, 0.48 19 $\frac{16}{25}$, 0.64 20 $\frac{18}{25}$, 0.72

21 $\frac{21}{25}$, 0.84 22 $\frac{9}{25}$, 0.36 23 $\frac{7}{25}$, 0.28 24 $\frac{3}{25}$, 0.12 25 $\frac{2}{25}$, 0.08

26 $\frac{3}{10}$, 0.3 27 $\frac{1}{10}$, 0.1 28 $\frac{3}{5}$, 0.6 29 $\frac{2}{5}$, 0.4 30 $\frac{1}{4}$, 0.25

Exercise 4.13 *page 47*

1 $\frac{1}{2}$, 50%   2 $\frac{31}{100}$, 31%   3 $\frac{2}{5}$, 40%   4 $\frac{1}{25}$, 4%   5 $\frac{4}{5}$, 80%

6 $\frac{2}{25}$, 8%   7 $\frac{9}{10}$, 90%   8 $\frac{9}{100}$, 9%   9 $\frac{1}{20}$, 5%   10 $\frac{23}{100}$, 23%

11 $\frac{8}{25}$, 32%   12 $\frac{99}{100}$, 99%   13 $\frac{1}{10}$, 10%   14 $\frac{1}{100}$, 1%   15 $\frac{3}{4}$, 75%

16 $\frac{29}{100}$, 29%   17 $\frac{23}{25}$, 92%   18 $\frac{1}{50}$, 2%   19 $\frac{1}{5}$, 20%   20 $\frac{19}{100}$, 19%

Exercise 4.14 *page 47*

1 0.31, 31%   2 0.27, 27%   3 0.87, 87%   4 0.99, 99%   5 0.03, 3%

6 0.01, 1%   7 0.18, 18%   8 0.42, 42%   9 0.38, 38%   10 0.54, 54%

11 0.45, 45%   12 0.65, 65%   13 0.95, 95%   14 0.16, 16%   15 0.24, 24%

16 0.04, 4%   17 0.32, 32%   18 0.44, 44%   19 0.52, 52%   20 0.56, 56%

21 0.68, 68%   22 0.7, 70%   23 0.8, 80%   24 0.75, 75%   25 0.5, 50%

Book 2   Unit 5

AT 2/4 (vii)   Pupils have begun to use simple formulae expressed in words.
AT 2/5 (vii)   Pupils construct, express in symbolic form, and use simple
formulae involving one or two operations.

Exercise 5.1 *page 48*

1 ab 2 mn 3 x^2 4 l^2 5 $6u$ 6 $10v$

7 $2xy$ 8 $3ab$ 9 $2ab$ 10 $3mn$ 11 $5xy$ 12 $6ab$

13 $10mn$ 14 $12pq$ 15 $9z^2$ 16 $16t^2$

Exercise 5.2 *page 49*

	a	b	c	d
1	24	60	$12x$	$24x$
2	30	60	$10x$	$30x$
3	100	150	$50x$	$200x$
4	60	100	$20y$	$200y$
5	80	200	$40y$	$200y$
6	300	600	$100x$	$400y$
7	50	75	$25x$	$50y$
8	30	60	$15p$	$60q$

Exercise 5.3 *page 50*

1 a $10x$ b $50x$ 2 a $10y$ b $120y$

3 a $100z$ b $200z$

4 a 120   b 300   c $60m$ d $300m$

5 a 500   b 1000   c $100n$ d $1000n$

6 $20a + 20b$

Exercise 5.4 *page 51*

1 $x + 5$ 2 $y + 5$ 3 $a + 2$ 4 $4 + x$ 5 $3 + p$

6 $2 + t$ 7 $y + x$ 8 $x + y$ 9 $q + p$ 10 $6 + 2p$

11 $5 + 3q$ 12 $9 + 4x$ 13 $5a + 6$ 14 $3b + 8$ 15 $7c + 5$

16 $3a + 2b$ 17 $5x + 2y$ 18 $4p + 7q$ 19 $x - 5$ 20 $y - 5$

21 $a - 2$ 22 $4 - x$ 23 $3 - p$ 24 $2 - t$ 25 $y - x$

26 $x - y$ 27 $q - p$ 28 $p - q$ 29 $5a - 6$ 30 $2b - 7$

31 $9c - 4$ 32 $3 - 2m$ 33 $8 - 5n$ 34 $7 - 3p$ 35 $10 - 9q$

36 $3a - 2b$ 37 $5p - 8q$ 38 $7x - 4y$ 39 $4b - 3a$ 40 $9n - 2m$

Exercise 5.5 *page 51*

1 7   2 8   3 11   4 6   5 6   6 10   7 5   8 4

9 8   10 7   11 12   12 10   13 5   14 12   15 10   16 6

17 6   18 19   19 1   20 8   21 1   22 1   23 20   24 2

25 2   26 18   27 2   28 9   29 16   30 0   31 11   32 12

33 23   34 1   35 15   36 12   37 7   38 8   39 14   40 3

41 18   42 11   43 13   44 25   45 27   46 1   47 10   48 3

49 3   50 30   51 16   52 9   53 20   54 8   55 9   56 40

57 3   58 3   59 500   60 0

page 2

Exercise 5.6   *page 52*

1 12	**2** 14	**3** 15	**4** 8	**5** 16	**6** 24	**7** 6	**8** 18
9 30	**10** 12	**11** 48	**12** 24	**13** 18	**14** 6	**15** 24	**16** 120
17 12	**18** 24	**19** 18	**20** 90	**21** 3	**22** 9	**23** 24	**24** 12
25 72	**26** 24	**27** 18	**28** 12	**29** 30	**30** 0	**31** 18	**32** 36
33 0	**34** 0	**35** 12	**36** 6	**37** 12	**38** 48	**39** 0	**40** 36
41 36	**42** 0	**43** 0	**44** 0				

$G \times 1$

Exercise 5.7   *page 52*

$Ex \times 2$

1 4	**2** 9	**3** 8	**4** 18	**5** 16	**6** 27	**7** 8	**8** 27
9 18	**10** 12	**11** 16	**12** 1	**13** 48	**14** 4	**15** 80	**16** 10
17 64	**18** 1	**19** 4	**20** 16				

Exercise 5.8   *page 53*

$\times 3$

1 12	**2** 30	**3** 6	**4** 10	**5** 4	**6** 2	**7** 24	**8** 36
9 13	**10** 5						

Exercise 5.9   *page 53*

1 $2a$	**2** $3b$	**3** $4c$	**4** $6d$	**5** $3l$	**6** $4m$	**7** $6n$	**8** $4p$
9 $7q$	**10** $9r$	**11** $5t$	**12** $8u$	**13** $10v$	**14** $7x$	**15** $11y$	**16** $10a$
17 $15b$	**18** $12c$	**19** $12m$	**20** $10n$	**21** $12l$	**22** $15p$	**23** $20q$	**24** $2a$
25 $3b$	**26** $5c$	**27** $6l$	**28** $9m$	**29** $3n$	**30** $8p$	**31** $11q$	**32** r
33 t	**34** u	**35** v	**36** $2a$	**37** $5b$	**38** $6c$	**39** $6l$	**40** m
41 0	**42** $3p$	**43** $2q$	**44** $4r$	**45** $4s$	**46** $3t$	**47** u	**48** v
49 x	**50** 0						

Exercise 5.10   *page 53*

1 $6x + 5y$	**2** $8u + 7v$	**3** $9a + 2b$	**4** $7x + 4y$	**5** $7m^2 + 3m$
6 $9n^2 + 8n$	**7** $3u + 4v$	**8** $2x + 9y$	**9** $7p + 9q$	**10** $l + 7m$
11 $3z^2 + 4z$	**12** $5a^2 + 6a$	**13** $8b^2 + 5b$	**14** $7m + 9n$	**15** $5p + 12q$
16 $3u + 8v$	**17** $5x^2 + 9x$	**18** $7y^2 + 9y$	**19** $5l + 3m$	**20** $12b + 7c$
21 $7q + 8r$	**22** $12a + 11b$	**23** $10t^2 + 3t$	**24** $12u^2 + 5u$	**25** $3x + 7y$
26 $4a + 9b$	**27** $m + 8n$	**28** $5p + 4q$	**29** $6u + 5v$	**30** $3z^2 + 2z$
31 $9a + 7b$	**32** $9x + 6y$	**33** $9p + 4q$	**34** $4c + 3d$	

Exercise 5.11   *page 54*

1 4	**2** 9	**3** 16	**4** 36	**5** 100
6 27	**7** 216	**8** 1000	**9** 125	**10** 1
11 16	**12** 32	**13** 64	**14** 16	**15** 36
16 100	**17** 81	**18** 81	**19** 135	**20** 225
21 900	**22** 1000	**23** 125	**24** 10 000	**25** 2500

Exercise 5.12   *page 54*

1 8^2	**2** 7^2	**3** 9^2	**4** 6^3	**5** 8^3
6 10^3	**7** 12^3	**8** a^2	**9** p^2	**10** t^2
11 b^3	**12** m^3	**13** z^3	**14** $2^2 \times 4^2$	**15** $3^2 \times 5^2$
16 $6^2 \times 10^2$	**17** $2^3 \times 7^2$	**18** $4^3 \times 9^2$	**19** $5^3 \times 6^2$	**20** $2^2 \times 5^3$
21 $8^2 \times 9^3$	**22** $x^2 \times y^2$	**23** $m^2 \times n^2$	**24** $u^2 \times v^2$	**25** $a^3 \times b^2$
26 $y^3 \times z^2$	**27** $u^3 \times v^2$	**28** $m^2 \times n^3$	**29** $p^2 \times q^3$	**30** $c^2 \times d^3$

Exercise 5.13   *page 54*

1 x^3	**2** y^3	**3** a^3	**4** b^3	**5** $6p^2$
6 $20q^2$	**7** $9r^2$	**8** $6s^2$	**9** $4x^3$	**10** $7y^3$
11 $3a^3$	**12** $9b^3$	**13** $15m^3$	**14** $12n^3$	**15** $16t^3$
16 $6u^3$	**17** $24v^3$	**18** $20z^3$	**19** $12a^3$	**20** $14b^3$
21 $24c^3$	**22** $9p^2$	**23** $16q^2$	**24** $4x^2$	**25** $100y^2$

Exercise 5.14   *page 55*

1 3	**2** 2	**3** 3	**4** 4	**5** 2	**6** 2	**7** 4	**8** 3
9 3	**10** 7	**11** 2	**12** 4	**13** 2	**14** 3	**15** 5	**16** 3
17 5	**18** 8	**19** 6	**20** 9				

Exercise 5.15	*page 55*								
		1 2	**2** 4	**3** 6	**4** 6	**5** 4	**6** 2	**7** 8	**8** 1
		9 3	**10** 6	**11** 5	**12** 2	**13** 5	**14** 5	**15** 7	**16** 1
		17 8	**18** 3	**19** 2	**20** 2	**21** 3	**22** 2	**23** 5	**24** 2
		25 6	**26** 2	**27** 5	**28** 2	**29** 3	**30** 1	**31** 4	**32** 5
		33 8	**34** 7	**35** 5	**36** 6	**37** 7	**38** 10	**39** 12	**40** 10

Exercise 5.16	*page 55*								
		1 3	**2** 5	**3** 6	**4** 7	**5** 8	**6** 9	**7** 3	**8** 20
		9 3	**10** 2	**11** 3	**12** 4	**13** 5	**14** 4	**15** 5	**16** 6
		17 4	**18** 5	**19** 4	**20** 9				

Exercise 5.17	*page 56*								
		1 3	**2** 4	**3** 6	**4** 1	**5** 2	**6** 4	**7** 5	**8** 1
		9 3	**10** 2	**11** 4	**12** 2	**13** 1	**14** 4	**15** 3	**16** 5
		17 6	**18** 4	**19** 4	**20** 5	**21** 2	**22** 5	**23** 3	**24** 2
		25 3	**26** 4	**27** 5	**28** 2	**29** 3	**30** 3		

Exercise 5.18	*page 56*							
		1 b	**2** a	**3** a	**4** c	**5** b	**6** a	**7** c
		8 b	**9** c	**10** a	**11** a	**12** b	**13** c	**14** b
		15 c	**16** a	**17** b	**18** a	**19** c	**20** b	**21** a

Book 2 Unit 6

AT 3/3 (ii)	Pupils use non-standard units and metric units of length, capacity,mass and time, in a range of contexts.
AT 3/5 (iii)	Pupils know the rough metric equivalents of Imperial units still in daily use and convert one metric unit to another. They make sensible estimates of a range of measures in relation to everyday situations.

Exercise 6.1	*page 57*				
		1 6 cm	**2** 8 cm	**3** 10 cm	**4** 5 cm, 50 mm
		5 35 mm	**6** 45 mm	**7** 25 mm	**8** 5 m, 3 m, 8 m
		9 14 m, 5 m, 9 m, 2 m, 1 m, 3 m		**10** 12 km, 17 km, 29 km	

Exercise 6.2	*page 59*				
		1 70 mm	**2** 160 mm	**3** 280 mm	**4** 400 mm
		5 19 cm	**6** 93 cm	**7** 6 cm	**8** 70 cm
		9 800 cm	**10** 4500 cm	**11** 23 600 cm	**12** 32 000 cm
		13 50 000 cm	**14** 3000 cm	**15** 72 m	**16** 518 m
		17 650 m	**18** 800 m	**19** 40 m	**20** 4000 m
		21 79 000 km	**22** 137 000 m	**23** 50 000 m	**24** 290 000 m
		25 100 000 m	**26** 42 km	**27** 215 km	**28** 80 km
		29 460 km	**30** 300 km	**31** 2 m 15 cm	**32** 6 m 32 cm
		33 3 m 4 cm	**34** 1 km 595 m	**35** 4 km 326 m	**36** 2 km 350 m
		37 3 km 400 m	**38** 5 km 76 m	**39** 5 cm 4 mm	**40** 7 cm 9 mm
		41 86 mm	**42** 98 mm	**43** 145 cm	**44** 372 cm
		45 507 cm	**46** 1870 m	**47** 2356 m	**48** 3058 m
		49 4080 m	**50** 1005 m		

Exercise 6.3	*page 59*				
		1 1 cm 9 mm	**2** 1 cm 4 mm	**3** 2 cm 3 mm	**4** 1 m 29 cm
		5 1 m 46 cm	**6** 1 m 18 cm	**7** 1 km 268 m	**8** 1 km 574 m
		9 1 km 142 m	**10** 1 km 64 m	**11** b	**12** a
		13 a	**14** c	**15** d	**16** a
		17 6 cm 9 mm	**18** 8 cm 2 mm	**19** 9 cm 5 mm	**20** 7 m 76 cm
		21 9 m 84 cm	**22** 9 m 62 cm	**23** 8 km 752 m	**24** 9 km 284 m

25	7 km 345 m	**26**	4 km 56 m	**27**	c	**28**	b
29	d	**30**	a	**31**	a	**32**	c

Exercise 6.4 *page 60*

1 4 mm	**2** 3 mm	**3** 1 cm 6 mm	**4** 3 cm 2 mm
5 44 cm	**6** 28 cm	**7** 3 m 65 cm	**8** 3 m 60 cm
9 4 m 96 cm	**10** 250 m	**11** 1 km 355 m	**12** 3 km 174 m
13 1 km 932 m	**14** 3 km 960 m	**15** 3 km 995 m	**16** 6 km 75 m
17 c	**18** a	**19** b	**20** b	**21** b
22 a	**23** b	**24** c	**25** a	

Exercise 6.5 *page 61*

1 4 m 10 cm, 5, 90 cm   **2** 70 cm   **3** 4 m 80 cm

Exercise 6.6 *page 62*

1 g	**2** kg	**3** g	**4** t	**5** g
6 kg	**7** kg	**8** t	**9** g	**10** kg

Exercise 6.7 *page 62*

1 5 kg	**2** 32 kg	**3** 8000 g	**4** 41 000 g
5 7 t	**6** 96 t	**7** 9000 kg	**8** 80 000 kg
9 2 kg 520 g	**10** 8 kg 75 g	**11** 4 t 372 kg	**12** 5 t 4 kg
13 3450 g	**14** 5032 g	**15** 6321 kg	**16** 2009 kg

Exercise 6.8 *page 63*

1 ml   **2** *l*   **3** *l*   **4** ml   **5** *l*   **6** *l*   **7** ml   **8** *l*   **9** ml   **10** *l*

Exercise 6.9 *page 63*

1 5 *l*	**2** 3.2 *l*	**3** 6.78 *l*	**4** 5.555 *l*	**5** 0.345 *l*
6 8000 *ml*	**7** 17 000 ml	**8** 2300 ml	**9** 3450 ml	**10** 934 ml

Exercise 6.10 *page 63*

1 a 280 mm **b** 28 cm		**2 a** 200 cm **b** 2 m	
3 a 400 cm **b** 4 m		**4 a** 2000 m **b** 2 km	
5 a 3000 g **b** 3 kg		**6 a** 8000 g **b** 8 kg	
7 yes	**8 a** 125 g **b** 8	**9** 36 g	**10** 5 g
11 85 g	**12** 2 t 300 kg	**13** 10 *l*	
14 a 330 ml or 0.33 *l* **b** 1.96 *l*		**15 a** 120 **b** 10 *l*	

Exercise 6.11 *page 66*

1 20 cm	**2** 6.25 cm	**3** 30 cm	**4** 45 cm
5 60 cm	**6** 90 cm	**7** 195 cm	**8** 450 cm
9 150 miles	**10** 200 miles	**11** 10 miles	**12** 30 miles
13 38 miles	**14** 188 miles	**15** 26 miles	**16** 96 miles

Exercise 6.12 *page 70*

1 10 kg	**2** 20 kg	**3** 70 kg	**4** 150 kg
5 650 kg	**6** 83.6 pounds	**7** 8.8 pounds	**8** 110 pounds
9 220 pounds	**10** 0.44 pounds	**11** 17.5 pints	**12** 26.25 pints
13 35 pints	**14** 52.5 pints	**15** 43.75 pints	

Book 2   Unit 7

AT 2/4 (viii)   Pupils use and interpret co-ordinates in the first quadrant.

Exercise 7.1 *page 73*

1 Barrhead (0, 10)	Coatbridge (25, 15)
Clydebank (0, 20)	Carron Bridge (25, 35)
Aberfoyle (0, 50)	Airdrie (30, 15)

Pollokshaws (5, 10)   Stirling (30, 45)
Milngavie (5, 25)   Dunblane (30, 50)
Balfron (5, 40)   Falkirk (40, 30)
Glasgow (10, 15)   Alloa (40, 45)
Fintry (10, 35)   Braehead (45, 0)
East Kilbride (15, 5)   Bathgate (45, 20)
Kirkintilloch (15, 25)   Linlithgow (50, 25)

2 Dean (1, 1)   Leroy (2, 4)   Luke (4, 3)
Lucy (1, 3)   Julie (2, 5)   Curt (4, 4)
Jack (1, 4)   David (3, 1)   Amy (5, 1)
Shaun (2, 1)   Will (3, 2)   Nat (5, 3)
Ken (2, 2)   Kay (3, 5)   Sam (5, 5)

3

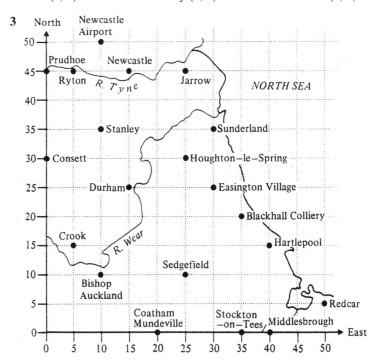

Exercise 7.2   *page 75*   A (0, 2),   B (0, 5),   C (1, 1),   D (1, 7),   E (2, 3),   F (2, 8),   G (3, 0),
H (3, 6),   I (4, 4),   J (4, 10),   K (5, 2),   L (5, 9),   M (6, 0),   N (6, 5),
P (7, 4),   Q (7, 7),   R (8, 1),   S (8, 9),   T (9, 3),   U (9, 10),   V (10, 6),
W (10, 8)

Exercise 7.3   *page 75*   **1** ship   **2** saucepan   **3** lamp   **4** aeroplane   **5** spade
6 key   **7** spanner   **8** British Rail sign
9 coat hanger   **10** traffic light

Exercise 7.4   *page 76*   **1** $x = 5$ **2** $x = 3$ **3** $x = 6$ **4** $y = 2$ **5** $y = 5$
6 $y = 1$ **7** $y = 0$ **8** $x + y = 4$ **9** $x + y = 6$ **10** $y = \frac{1}{2}x$

Exercise 7.5   *page 78*   **1 a** 6.4   **b** 1.8   **2 a** 1.2   **b** 7.6
3 a 156°   **b** 108°   **c** 36°   **d** 12°
4 a 84 p   **b** 58 p   **c** 46 p   **d** 24 p

5	**a** 5	**b** 1.2			**6**	**a** 5	**b** 1.6	
7	**a** 45	**b** 20	**c** 15		**8**	**a** 32 cm	**b** 16 cm	
10	4 and 2				**11**	$4\frac{1}{2}$ and $1\frac{1}{2}$, or 4.5 and 1.5		

Exercise 7.6 *page 80*

1 **a** 60 cm, 140 cm, 180 cm, 220 cm   **b** sixth, eighth, twelfth, fourteenth
2 **a** 11 cm, 15 cm, 18 cm, 21 cm   **b** 20 g, 35 g, 50 g
3 **a** 4 mm, 12 mm, 32 mm   **b** 200, 300, 450
4 **a** 200 g, 800 g, 1200 g   **b** 150, 400, 450
5 **a** 150, 168   **b** 480 g
6 **a** BF 30, BF 120, BF 210, BF 450
   b £2.50, £4, £6.50
7 90 p, £1.08, £1.44   8 210 cm, 162 cm
9 **a** 65 mm, 80 mm   **b** 150 cm, 170 cm
10 40%, 55%, 70%, 3, 5, 16

Book 2   Unit 8

AT 4/4 (ii)	Pupils understand and use the mode and the median.
AT 4/5 (i)	Pupils understand and use the mean of discrete data.
AT 4/5 (ii)	Pupils compare two simple distributions, using the range and one of the measures of average.

Exercise 8.1 *page 82*

1 11	**2** 9	**3** 25	**4** 95	**5** 53 cm
6 75 kg	**7** 59 g	**8** 48 p	**9** £33	**10** £2
11 £175	**12** £8	**13** £1	**14** £33	**15** 2 m
16 1 m	**17** £272	**18** 13 years	**19** 11 years	**20** 15
21 44	**22** 9 kg	**23** 12 cm	**24** 10 cm	

25 **a** 13   **b** 14   **c** 135   **d** 27

Exercise 8.2 *page 83*

1 18.4	**2** 29.2	**3** 13.5 g	**4** £7.50
5 14.5 kg	**6** £13.60	**7** 3.5	**8** 6.5 m
9 £2.16	**10** 99 p	**11** 30.5	**12** 1 m 78 cm
13 £375.20	**14** £27.60	**15** 17 cm 4 mm	**16** 11 cm 7 mm
17 21 kg 600 g	**18** 9 l 950 ml		

Exercise 8.3 *page 84*

1 21	**2** 110	**3** 4, 2	**4** 3	**5** 18
6 4	**7** 61	**8** 13, 11	**9** 10	**10** 105
11 3	**12** 2	**13** 1 h	**14** 2 h	**15** 45 857

Exercise 8.4 *page 85*

1 15   **2** 1   **3** 4   **4** 2   **5** 4   **6** 5   **7** 1   **8** 25   **9** 17   **10** 2

Exercise 8.5 *page 86*

1 5	**2** 16 litres	**3** 33	**4** 58.5 p	**5** 19, 10
6 22 °C	**7** 53 km	**8** 200	**9** 41 days	**10** 17

Exercise 8.6 *page 87*

1 mean	**2** mode	**3** median	**4** mean
5 median	**6** median	**7** mean	**8** mode

Exercise 8.7 *page 88*

1 8   **2** 37   **3** 14   **4** 9   **5** 9   **6** 6   **7** 3   **8** 1   **9** 0.4   **10** 8

Exercise 8.8 *page 89*

1 a Striko   mean = 40.2
                      range = 7
          Katchwell   mean = 40.9
                      range = 16

2 a Amarjit   mean = 14.24
                      range = 49
          Martha   mean = 9.4
                      range = 15

3 a Bill   mean = 58.3
                      range = 184
          Ted   mean = 56.75
                      range = 91

4 a London   median = 52.9 p
                      range = 13 p
          Newcastle   median = 50.4 p
                      range = 7 p

5 a TooCool   median = 197 °C
                      range = 5 °C
          Burnall   median = 200 °C
                      range = 10 °C

Book 3 Unit 1

AT 2/3 (ii) (part) Pupils have begun to recognise negative numbers in contexts such as money, temperature and calculator displays.

AT 2/5 (ii) Pupils order, add and subtract negative numbers in context.

Exercise 1.1 *page 1*

1 15 °C	**2** 19 °C	**3** 15 °C	**4** 12 °C	**5** 13 °C
6 11 °C	**7** +2°	**8** −4°	**9** −7°	**10** 8 °C
11 11 °C	**12** −6 °C	**13** −2 °C	**14** −1 °C	**15** −6°
16 −5°	**17** 2 °C	**18** 5 °C	**19** 4 °C	**20** 3 °C
21 +9°	**22** +6°	**23** −2 °C	**24** −1 °C	**25** −7 °C
26 −9 °C	**27** −2°	**28** −6°	**29** −3 °C	**30** −4 °C

Exercise 1.2 *page 2*

1 £740	**2** £1910	**3** £39	**4** £1040	**5** £675
6 £0	**7** £100	**8** £17	**9** £200	**10** £370
11 −£150	**12** −£1	**13** −£196	**14** −£100	**15** −£70
16 −£109	**17** −£676	**18** −£400	**19** −£103	**20** −£1187

Exercise 1.3 *page 3*

1 5	**2** −1	**3** 1	**4** −5	**5** 5
6 1	**7** −1	**8** −5	**9** 20	**10** −2
11 2	**12** −20	**13** 14	**14** 4	**15** −4
16 −14	**17** 2	**18** 0	**19** 0	**20** −2

Exercise 1.4 *page 3*

1

add	6	4	2	0	−2	−4	−6
4	10	8	6	4	2	0	−2
2	8	6	4	2	0	−2	−4
0	6	4	2	0	−2	−4	−6
−2	4	2	0	−2	−4	−6	−8
−4	2	0	−2	−4	−6	−8	−10
−6	0	−2	−4	−6	−8	−10	−12

2

add	9	6	3	0	−3	−6	−9
6	15	12	9	6	3	0	−3
3	12	9	6	3	0	−3	−6
0	9	6	3	0	−3	−6	−9
−3	6	3	0	−3	−6	−9	−12
−6	3	0	−3	−6	−9	−12	−15
−9	0	−3	−6	−9	−12	−15	−18

3

add	5	3	2	0	−2	−3	−5
2	7	5	4	2	0	−1	−3
0	5	3	2	0	−2	−3	−5
−2	3	1	0	−2	−4	−5	−7
−3	2	0	−1	−3	−5	−6	−8
−5·	0	−2	−3	−5	−7	−8	−10
−7	−2	−4	−5	−7	−9	−10	−12

Exercise 1.5   *page 4*

1 8	**2** 15	**3** 16	**4** −8	**5** −14
6 −4	**7** −15	**8** −10	**9** −11	**10** −14
11 −16	**12** −7	**13** −15	**14** −6x	**15** −11y
16 −8z	**17** −6a	**18** −13b	**19** −14c	**20** −13d

Exercise 1.6   *page 4*

1 6	**2** 4	**3** 5	**4** 15	**5** 4x
6 8y	**7** 8z	**8** 4	**9** 2	**10** 6
11 6a	**12** 4b	**13** 3c	**14** −3	**15** −6
16 −8	**17** −6	**18** −4p	**19** −7q	**20** −r
21 −2	**22** −5	**23** −7	**24** −4u	

Exercise 1.7   *page 4*

1

take → / from ↓	4	3	2	1	0	−1	−2
6	2	3	4	5	6	7	8
3	−1	0	1	2	3	4	5
0	−4	−3	−2	−1	0	1	2
−3	−7	−6	−5	−4	−3	−2	−1

2

take → / from ↓	6	4	2	0	−2	−4	−6
12	6	8	10	12	14	16	18
6	0	2	4	6	8	10	12
0	−6	−4	−2	0	2	4	6
−3	−12	−10	−8	−6	−4	−2	0

3

take → / from ↓	12	9	6	3	0	−3	−6
12	0	3	6	9	12	15	18
6	−6	−3	0	3	6	9	12
0	−12	−9	−6	−3	0	3	6
−6	−18	−15	−12	−9	−6	−3	0

4

take → / from ↓	4	3	2	1	0	−1	−2
4	0	1	2	3	4	5	6
0	−4	−3	−2	−1	0	1	2
−4	−8	−7	−6	−5	−4	−3	−2
−8	−12	−11	−10	−9	−8	−7	−6

5 take → / from ↓

take → from ↓	4	3	2	1	0	−1	−2
2	−2	−1	0	1	2	3	4
0	−4	−3	−2	−1	0	1	2
−2	−6	−5	−4	−3	−2	−1	0
−4	−8	−7	−6	−5	−4	−3	−2

6 take → / from ↓

take → from ↓	15	10	5	0	−5	−10	−15
10	−5	0	5	10	15	20	25
5	−10	−5	0	5	10	15	20
0	−15	−10	−5	0	5	10	15
−5	−20	−15	−10	−5	0	5	10

Exercise 1.8 *page 5*

1 4	**2** 7	**3** $2x$	**4** $6y$	**5** -2
6 -5	**7** $-5z$	**8** $-6t$	**9** $-2u$	**10** $-v$
11 -5	**12** -15	**13** -14	**14** $-11p$	**15** $-10q$
16 -9	**17** -17	**18** $-13a$	**19** $-15b$	**20** $-16c$

Exercise 1.9 *page 5*

1 7	**2** 12	**3** $11x$	**4** $12y$	**5** 10
6 15	**7** $10z$	**8** $18t$	**9** 4	**10** 1
11 3	**12** 7	**13** $5a$	**14** $2b$	**15** $8c$
16 d	**17** -3	**18** -2	**19** -5	**20** $-6x$
21 $-6y$	**22** $-4z$	**23** $-5t$	**24** $-4u$	**25** $-v$

Book 3   Unit 2

AT 2/5 (iii)	Pupils use all four operations with decimals in two places.
AT 2/6 (i)	Pupils order and approximate decimals when solving numerical problems and equations such as $x^2 = 20$, using trial-and-improvement methods.
AT 2/7 (i)	In making estimates, pupils round to one significant figure and multiply and divide mentally.
AT 3/7 (v)	Pupils appreciate the continuous nature of measurement and recognise that a measurement given to the nearest whole number may be inaccurate by up to one half in either direction.
AT 3/7 (v)	Pupils understand and use compound measures, such as speed.

Exercise 2.1 *page 6*

1 64.62	64.52	64.52	**a**		**2** 32.31	32.41	32.31	**b**
3 54.65	54.75	54.65	**b**		**4** 28.34	28.34	28.24	**c**
5 25.76	25.86	25.86	**c**		**6** 14.85	14.75	14.75	**a**
7 15.46	15.46	15.36	**c**		**8** 3.24	3.14	3.24	**b**
9 3.36	3.26	3.26	**a**		**10** 6.42	6.52	6.42	**b**

Exercise 2.2 *page 6*

1 1.4	**2** 3.2	**3** 5.4	**4** 12.8	**5** 11.5
6 25.6	**7** 1.35	**8** 1.68	**9** 2.82	**10** 0.63
11 0.4	**12** 0.08	**13** 0.24	**14** 0.42	**15** 0.3
16 0.09	**17** 0.192	**18** 0.165	**19** 0.008	**20** 0.006
21 0.015	**22** 0.65	**23** 0.64	**24** 0.91	**25** 1.92
26 1.8	**27** 0.372	**28** 0.384	**29** 0.624	**30** 0.66

Exercise 2.3 *page 6*

1 3.22	**2** 5.12	**3** 6.45	**4** 3.78	**5** 4.68	**6** 5.25
7 3.6	**8** 8.4	**9** 13.12	**10** 11.76	**11** 13.95	**12** 12.72
13 10.08	**14** 13.2	**15** 16	**16** 0.448	**17** 0.585	**18** 0.432
19 0.756	**20** 0.588	**21** 0.864	**22** 0.696	**23** 0.72	**24** 1.472

Exercise 2.4 *page 7*

1 3.4	**2** 3.8	**3** 2.9	**4** 2.6	**5** 3.4	**6** 4.4
7 5.3	**8** 4.5	**9** 1.6	**10** 1.7	**11** 1.3	**12** 2.9
13 2.4	**14** 0.9	**15** 0.5	**16** 0.8	**17** 0.7	**18** 0.6
19 0.8	**20** 0.9	**21** 0.6	**22** 0.5	**23** 1.5	**24** 1.6

Exercise 2.5 *page 7*

1 17.6	**2** 14.5	**3** 12.2	**4** 10.6	**5** 16.1	**6** 18
7 26	**8** 14.5	**9** 19.2	**10** 6.7	**11** 8.6	**12** 7.2
13 8.6	**14** 1.3	**15** 1.4	**16** 1.8	**17** 1.5	**18** 17
19 38	**20** 34	**21** 28	**22** 35	**23** 34	**24** 20
25 1.3	**26** 1.2	**27** 1.9	**28** 0.8	**29** 0.7	**30** 0.9

Exercise 2.6 *page 8*

1 £27	**2** 3 kg	**3** 9 m, £10.80	
4 a 94.8 kg	**b** 66 kg	**c** 16.5 kg	
5 200 g	**6** 1 litre	**7** 9.6 cm	**8** 15
9 25	**10** 6	**11** 0.9 kg	
12 a 3.5 m	**b** 2.5 m	**c** 6.4 m^2	

Exercise 2.7 *page 9*

1 b	**2** c	**3** b	**4** a	**5** a	**6** c	**7** a	**8** c
9 b	**10** b	**11** a	**12** b	**13** c	**14** b	**15** a	**16** c

Exercise 2.8 *page 9*

1 a 172.8	**b** 172.8	**c** 1728	
2 a 43.2	**b** 43.2	**c** 432	
3 a 49	**b** 49	**c** 490	
4 a 90	**b** 90	**c** 900	
5 a 19.38	**b** 19.38	**c** 1938	
6 a 3.36	**b** 3.36	**c** 336	
7 a 18	**b** 18	**c** 1800	
8 a 1.296	**b** 1.296	**c** 12.96	
9 a 0.276	**b** 0.276	**c** 2.76	**d** 2.76	**e** 2.76	**f** 276
10 a 0.54	**b** 0.54	**c** 5.4	**d** 5.4	**e** 5.4	**f** 540

Exercise 2.9 *page 10*

1 0.375	**2** 0.3	**3** 0.7	**4** 0.4	**5** 0.8
6 0.45	**7** 0.55	**8** 0.225	**9** 0.425	**10** 0.175
11 0.025	**12** 0.22	**13** 0.82	**14** 0.3125	**15** 0.5625

Exercise 2.10 *page 10*

1 0.$\dot{6}$	**2** 0.$\dot{3}$	**3** 0.8$\dot{3}$	**4** 0.1$\dot{6}$	**5** 0.41$\dot{6}$
6 0.58$\dot{3}$	**7** 0.91$\dot{6}$	**8** 0.08$\dot{3}$	**9** 0.$\dot{4}$	**10** 0.$\dot{7}$
11 0.$\dot{1}$	**12** 0.5$\dot{4}$	**13** 0.2$\dot{7}$	**14** 0.2$\dot{3}$	**15** 0.4$\dot{3}$

Exercise 2.11   *page 10*

	a	b	c
1	£17.90	£18.00	£20.00
2	£36.90	£37.00	£40.00
3	£57.10	£57.00	£60.00
4	£42.40	$42.00	£40.00
5	£63.30	£63.00	£60.00
6	£24.80	£25.00	£20.00
7	£38.20	£38.00	£40.00
8	£14.50	£15.00	£10.00
9	£53.00	£53.00	£50.00
10	£49.80	£50.00	£50.00
11	£26.10	£26.00	£30.00
12	£30.80	£31.00	£30.00

Exercise 2.12   *page 11*

1 1.4   2 4.6   3 5.6   4 3.4
5 6.3   6 8.8   7 7.9   8 8.1
9 0.9   10 5.1   11 2.0   12 5.0
13 1.54   14 3.95   15 2.62   16 6.58
17 4.29   18 0.89   19 5.97   20 1.66
21 6.12   22 4.51   23 3.40   24 2.01
25 1.40   26 5.70   27 5.00   28 2.00
29 1.3   30 2.5   31 5.4   32 4.7
33 3.9   34 2.1   35 0.9   36 1.4
37 5.0   38 5.0

39 a 4.37 b 4.4   40 a 2.54 b 2.5
41 a 1.72 b 1.7   42 a 0.58 b 0.6
43 a 5.25 b 5.3   44 a 6.87 b 6.9
45 a 1.40 b 1.4   46 a 4.98 b 5.0
47 a 3.00 b 3.0   48 a 3.02 b 3.0
49 a 4.04 b 4.0   50 a 5.07 b 5.1
51 a 1.09 b 1.1   52 a 2.41 b 2.4
53 a 3.20 b 3.2   54 a 4.01 b 4.0
55 a 5.00 b 5.0   56 a 6.10 b 6.1
57 a 1.06 b 1.1   58 a 0.56 b 0.6

Exercise 2.13   *page 11*

1 1.8   2 70.0   3 2.2   4 95.3
5 29.7   6 6.7   7 588.8   8 513.6
9 23.3   10 0.7   11 5.9   12 4.8
13 93.6   14 48.5   15 0.2   16 7.7
17 21.8   18 159.1   19 0.8   20 48.2
21 0.71   22 903.94   23 0.73   24 27.02
25 1.78   26 0.61   27 14.77   28 97.27
29 764.42   30 456.97   31 382.42   32 0.22
33 2.18   34 0.44   35 0.01   36 0.00
37 7.11   38 15.36   39 0.18   40 53.41

Exercise 2.14   *page 12*

1 a £8.67 b £1.78 c £2.66 d £3.99 e £2.33
   f £4.33 g £5.06 h £11.87 i £2.60 j £7.19
2 a 96p b £1.07 c 67p d £1.91 e £2.78
   f £1.45 g £1.84 h £2.01 i £3.33 j £4.95
3 a £49 285.71 b £72 727.27 c £411 518.33
   d £346 043.12 e £14.77 f £2048.56
   g £1 013 764.70 h £5 112 845.77 i £1407.89
   j £61 911.11

4 **a** £3.72   **b** £3.83   **c** £5.08   **d** £5.82   **e** £4.67
   f £5.81   **g** £5.01   **h** £6.23   **i** £6.49

Exercise 2.15 *page 13*

1	0.33	**2**	0.67	**3**	0.5	**4**	0.17	**5**	0.2
6	0.8	**7**	0.4	**8**	0.6	**9**	0.1	**10**	0.3
11	0.9	**12**	0.08	**13**	0.42	**14**	0.92	**15**	0.75
16	0.07	**17**	0.13	**18**	0.05	**19**	0.15	**20**	0.45

Exercise 2.16 *page 13*

1	$50\,\text{km}\,\text{h}^{-1}$	**2**	$60\,\text{km}\,\text{h}^{-1}$	**3**	$55\,\text{km}\,\text{h}^{-1}$	**4**	$84\,\text{km}\,\text{h}^{-1}$
5	$63\,\text{km}\,\text{h}^{-1}$	**6**	$82\,\text{km}\,\text{h}^{-1}$	**7**	$134\,\text{km}\,\text{h}^{-1}$	**8**	$118\,\text{km}\,\text{h}^{-1}$
9	$103\,\text{km}\,\text{h}^{-1}$	**10**	$105\,\text{km}\,\text{h}^{-1}$	**11**	$40\,\text{km}\,\text{h}^{-1}$	**12**	$80\,\text{km}\,\text{h}^{-1}$
13	$60\,\text{km}\,\text{h}^{-1}$	**14**	$100\,\text{km}\,\text{h}^{-1}$	**15**	$50\,\text{km}\,\text{h}^{-1}$	**16**	$72\,\text{km}\,\text{h}^{-1}$
17	$120\,\text{km}\,\text{h}^{-1}$	**18**	$80\,\text{km}\,\text{h}^{-1}$	**19**	$40\,\text{km}\,\text{h}^{-1}$	**20**	$120\,\text{km}\,\text{h}^{-1}$

Exercise 2.17 *page 14*

1	$100\,\text{km}\,\text{h}^{-1}$	**2**	$48\,\text{km}\,\text{h}^{-1}$	**3**	$72\,\text{km}\,\text{h}^{-1}$	**4**	$60\,\text{km}\,\text{h}^{-1}$
5	$84\,\text{km}\,\text{h}^{-1}$	**6**	$100\,\text{km}\,\text{h}^{-1}$	**7**	$75\,\text{km}\,\text{h}^{-1}$	**8**	$96\,\text{km}\,\text{h}^{-1}$
9	$54\,\text{km}\,\text{h}^{-1}$	**10**	$72\,\text{km}\,\text{h}^{-1}$	**11**	$48\,\text{km}\,\text{h}^{-1}$	**12**	$70\,\text{km}\,\text{h}^{-1}$
13	$135\,\text{km}\,\text{h}^{-1}$	**14**	$108\,\text{km}\,\text{h}^{-1}$	**15**	$92\,\text{km}\,\text{h}^{-1}$	**16**	$140\,\text{km}\,\text{h}^{-1}$
17	$60\,\text{km}\,\text{h}^{-1}$	**18**	$42\,\text{km}\,\text{h}^{-1}$	**19**	$39\,\text{km}\,\text{h}^{-1}$	**20**	$32\,\text{km}\,\text{h}^{-1}$

Exercise 2.18 *page 14*

1	240 km	**2**	360 km	**3**	450 km	**4**	360 km	**5**	170 km
6	385 km	**7**	500 km	**8**	423 km	**9**	540 km	**10**	75 km
11	200 km	**12**	180 km	**13**	200 km	**14**	70 km	**15**	180 km
16	440 km	**17**	16 km	**18**	90 km	**19**	105 km	**20**	90 km
21	105 km	**22**	210 km	**23**	162 km	**24**	120 km	**25**	80 km
26	147 km	**27**	24 km	**28**	63 km	**29**	16 km	**30**	60 km
31	300 km	**32**	375 km	**33**	846 km	**34**	192 km	**35**	231 km
36	80 km	**37**	63 km	**38**	36 km	**39**	18 km	**40**	360 km

Exercise 2.19 *page 15*

1	3 h	**2**	4 h	**3**	8 h	**4**	5 h
5	6 h	**6**	7 h	**7**	4 h	**8**	8 h
9	5 h	**10**	3 h	**11**	6 h	**12**	4 h
13	7 h	**14**	9 h	**15**	1 h 30 min	**16**	2 h 30 min
17	3 h 30 min	**18**	4 h 30 min	**19**	1 h 15 min	**20**	1 h 45 min
21	2 h 15 min	**22**	2 h 45 min	**23**	1 h 20 min	**24**	1 h 40 min
25	2 h 20 min	**26**	2 h 40 min	**27**	15 min	**28**	45 min
29	20 min	**30**	40 min	**31**	5 h	**32**	6 h
33	9 h	**34**	4 h 30 min	**35**	2 h 30 min	**36**	1 h 45 min
37	1 h 40 min	**38**	2 h 15 min	**39**	15 min	**40**	40 min

Exercise 2.20 *page 16*

1	<u>34</u>	**2**	<u>506</u>	**3**	<u>6</u>.7	**4**	0.<u>5</u>5
5	<u>6</u>.09	**6**	0.0<u>5</u>	**7**	0.00<u>1</u> 09	**8**	<u>1</u>000.6
9	<u>1</u>999	**10**	0.00<u>4</u>	**11**	0.0<u>1</u>0 101	**12**	0.000 0<u>1</u>0 999
13	<u>1</u>20 000	**14**	0.00<u>1</u>2	**15**	<u>1</u>0 000	**16**	0.00<u>1</u> 07

Exercise 2.21 *page 16*

1	68	**2**	78	**3**	56	**4**	76	**5**	40
6	24	**7**	93	**8**	13	**9**	21	**10**	68
11	3.1	**12**	7.9	**13**	4.5	**14**	4.2	**15**	5.1
16	5.4	**17**	1.5	**18**	1.5	**19**	6.0	**20**	0.57
21	0.83	**22**	0.86	**23**	0.68	**24**	0.63	**25**	0.046
26	0.032	**27**	0.037	**28**	0.071	**29**	0.073	**30**	35
31	34	**32**	78	**33**	6.7	**34**	0.0043	**35**	18

Exercise 2.22 *page 16*	**1** 375	**2** 374	**3** 734	**4** 735	**5** 537
	6 7.89	**7** 6.63	**8** 6.26	**9** 6.13	**10** 9.02
	11 0.0362	**12** 0.0458	**13** 0.005 56	**14** 0.002 20	**15** 0.000 152
	16 6	**17** 8	**18** 8	**19** 7	**20** 7
	21 6	**22** 3	**23** 3	**24** 3	**25** 3
	26 0.05	**27** 0.05	**28** 0.006	**29** 0.006	**30** 0.04

Exercise 2.23 *page 17*

1 All answers to 3 sf.

a 2350	**b** 2350	**c** 2450	**d** 2440	**e** 2540	**f** 2530
g 3250	**h** 3250	**i** 3450	**j** 3430	**k** 1260	**l** 10 000
m 346	**n** 3460	**o** 9010	**p** 10 600	**q** 87 500	**r** 87 900
s 88 900	**t** 44 400	**u** 33 300	**v** 152 000	**w** 223 000	**x** 668 000

2 All answers to 2 sf.

a 2300	**b** 2400	**c** 2500	**d** 2400	**e** 2500	**f** 2500
g 3200	**h** 3300	**i** 3500	**j** 3400	**k** 1300	**l** 10 000
m 350	**n** 3500	**o** 9000	**p** 11 000	**q** 87 000	**r** 88 000
s 89 000	**t** 44 000	**u** 33 000	**v** 150 000	**w** 220 000	**x** 670 000

3 All answers to 1 sf.

a 2000	**b** 2000	**c** 2000	**d** 2000	**e** 3000	**f** 3000
g 3000	**h** 3000	**i** 3000	**j** 3000	**k** 1000	**l** 10 000
m 300	**n** 3000	**o** 9000	**p** 10 000	**q** 90 000	**r** 90 000
s 90 000	**t** 40 000	**u** 30 000	**v** 200 000	**w** 200 000	**x** 700 000

Exercise 2.24 *page 17*

1 20, 25.1	**2** 10, 9.6	**3** 90, 111.0
4 90, 72.5	**5** 400, 341.7	**6** 10, 14.1
7 2000, 1952.5	**8** 200, 218.4	**9** 70, 76.0
10 100, 97.4	**11** 6000, 5964.5	**12** 30, 26.6
13 60 000, 57 835.8	**14** 10, 9.9	**15** 9000, 10 384.5
16 20, 14.9	**17** 4000, 5745.3	**18** 7, 5.5
19 300, 296.3	**20** 5, 5.6	**21** 10, 13.4
22 90, 106.4	**23** 50, 52.7	**24** 10, 11.8
25 2, 1.9	**26** 30, 28.0	**27** 1, 1.1
28 1, 1.0	**29** 50, 57.2	**30** 20, 16.4

31 a £4000	**b** £4062.50		
32 a 10 m^2	**b** £80	**c** £84.80	
33 a 30 *l*	**b** £10	**c** £11.00	
34 a 50 mph	**b** 57.3 mph		
35 a £60	**b** £50.08		

Exercise 2.25 *page 18*

1 1.5 kg, 2.5 kg	**2** 99.5 m, 100.5 m	**3** 99.5 cm, 100.5 cm
4 64.5 min, 65.5 min	**5** 59.5 cm^2, 60.5 cm^2	**6** 55.5 mm, 56.5 mm
7 54.5 g, 55.5 g	**8** 449.5 g, 500.5 g	**9** 2.5 min, 3.5 min
10 24.5 m^2, 25.5 m^2		

Exercise 2.26 *page 19*

1 a 49.5 cm	**b** 50.5 cm	**c** 89.5 cm	**d** 90.5 cm
e 4430.25 cm^2	**f** 4570.25 cm^2		
2 a 59.5 mph	**b** 60.5 mph	**c** 239.5 miles	**d** 240.5 miles
e 4.04 h	**f** 3.96 h		
3 a 24.5 m	**b** 25.5 m	**c** 2450 cm	**d** 2550 cm
e 79.5 cm	**f** 80.5 cm	**g** 30	**h** 32
4 a 199.5 mm	**b** 200.5 mm	**c** 478 002 mm^2	**d** 482 002 mm^2
5 a 54.5 m	**b** 55.5 m	**c** 2970.25 m^2	**d** 3080.25 m^2
e 47	**f** 49		

Book 3   Unit 3

AT 3/4 (ii)	Pupils draw common 2-D shapes in different orientations on grids.
AT 3/4 (iii)	Pupils identify congruent shapes.

Translations are not specifically mentioned in the Attainment Target but are included in the Programme of Study under Shape, Space and Measures:
3b Pupils should be taught to recognise and visualise the transformations of translation, reflection, rotation and enlargement, and their combination in two dimensions; understand the notations used to describe them.

Exercise 3.1   *page 20*

1 $\begin{pmatrix} -6 \\ 4 \end{pmatrix}$ 2 $\begin{pmatrix} 8 \\ 4 \end{pmatrix}$ 3 $\begin{pmatrix} 4 \\ 2 \end{pmatrix}$ 4 $\begin{pmatrix} 4 \\ 7 \end{pmatrix}$ 5 $\begin{pmatrix} -6 \\ -4 \end{pmatrix}$

6 $\begin{pmatrix} 6 \\ -4 \end{pmatrix}$ 7 $\begin{pmatrix} 0 \\ -4 \end{pmatrix}$ 8 $\begin{pmatrix} 6 \\ -4 \end{pmatrix}$ 9 $\begin{pmatrix} 14 \\ 0 \end{pmatrix}$ 10 $\begin{pmatrix} 10 \\ -2 \end{pmatrix}$

11 $\begin{pmatrix} 10 \\ 3 \end{pmatrix}$ 12 $\begin{pmatrix} 0 \\ -8 \end{pmatrix}$ 13 $\begin{pmatrix} 12 \\ -8 \end{pmatrix}$ 14 $\begin{pmatrix} 6 \\ -8 \end{pmatrix}$ 15 $\begin{pmatrix} -8 \\ -4 \end{pmatrix}$

16 $\begin{pmatrix} -14 \\ 0 \end{pmatrix}$ 17 $\begin{pmatrix} -4 \\ -2 \end{pmatrix}$ 18 $\begin{pmatrix} -4 \\ 3 \end{pmatrix}$ 19 $\begin{pmatrix} -14 \\ -8 \end{pmatrix}$ 20 $\begin{pmatrix} -2 \\ -8 \end{pmatrix}$

21 $\begin{pmatrix} -8 \\ -8 \end{pmatrix}$ 22 $\begin{pmatrix} -4 \\ -2 \end{pmatrix}$ 23 $\begin{pmatrix} -10 \\ 2 \end{pmatrix}$ 24 $\begin{pmatrix} 4 \\ 2 \end{pmatrix}$ 25 $\begin{pmatrix} 0 \\ 5 \end{pmatrix}$

26 $\begin{pmatrix} -10 \\ -6 \end{pmatrix}$ 27 $\begin{pmatrix} 2 \\ -6 \end{pmatrix}$ 28 $\begin{pmatrix} -4 \\ -6 \end{pmatrix}$ 29 $\begin{pmatrix} -4 \\ -7 \end{pmatrix}$ 30 $\begin{pmatrix} -10 \\ -3 \end{pmatrix}$

31 $\begin{pmatrix} 4 \\ -3 \end{pmatrix}$ 32 $\begin{pmatrix} 0 \\ -5 \end{pmatrix}$ 33 $\begin{pmatrix} -10 \\ -11 \end{pmatrix}$ 34 $\begin{pmatrix} 2 \\ -11 \end{pmatrix}$ 35 $\begin{pmatrix} -4 \\ -11 \end{pmatrix}$

36 $\begin{pmatrix} 6 \\ 4 \end{pmatrix}$ 37 $\begin{pmatrix} 0 \\ 8 \end{pmatrix}$ 38 $\begin{pmatrix} 14 \\ 8 \end{pmatrix}$ 39 $\begin{pmatrix} 10 \\ 6 \end{pmatrix}$ 40 $\begin{pmatrix} 10 \\ 11 \end{pmatrix}$

41 $\begin{pmatrix} 12 \\ 0 \end{pmatrix}$ 42 $\begin{pmatrix} 6 \\ 0 \end{pmatrix}$

Exercise 3.5   *page 24*

1 $\begin{pmatrix} 2 \\ 4 \end{pmatrix}$ 2 $\begin{pmatrix} 3 \\ 4 \end{pmatrix}$ 3 $\begin{pmatrix} 2 \\ 2 \end{pmatrix}$ 4 $\begin{pmatrix} 3 \\ 0 \end{pmatrix}$

5 $\begin{pmatrix} 2 \\ 1 \end{pmatrix}$ 6 $\begin{pmatrix} 3 \\ -4 \end{pmatrix}$ 7 $\begin{pmatrix} 1 \\ -4 \end{pmatrix}$ 8 $\begin{pmatrix} 0 \\ -2 \end{pmatrix}$

9 $\begin{pmatrix} -2 \\ 3 \end{pmatrix}$ 10 $\begin{pmatrix} -4 \\ 3 \end{pmatrix}$ 11 $\begin{pmatrix} -3 \\ 3 \end{pmatrix}$ 12 $\begin{pmatrix} -3 \\ -1 \end{pmatrix}$

Exercise 3.6   *page 26*

1 **a, b** and **d**	2 **a** and **b**	3 **b, c** and **d**
4 **a, b** and **c**	5 **a, b, c** and **d**	6 **b** and **c**
7 **a, b** and **d**	8 **a** and **d**	9 **a, b, c** and **d**
10 **b** and **d**	11 **a, b** and **d**	12 **a, b, c** and **d**

Exercise 3.7 *page 29*

1 A to E   reflection in the line $y = 4$

   B to C   translation $\begin{pmatrix} 2 \\ 0 \end{pmatrix}$

   D to F   rotation $-90°$ about $(4, 0)$

2 A to F   translation $\begin{pmatrix} 8 \\ -4 \end{pmatrix}$

   B to C   rotation $90°$ about $(1, 6)$
   D to E   reflection in the line $y = 5$

3 A to B   rotation $180°$ about $(5, 7)$
   C to F   reflection in the line $x = 5$

   D to E   translation $\begin{pmatrix} 4 \\ 1 \end{pmatrix}$

4 A to D   translation $\begin{pmatrix} 5 \\ -3 \end{pmatrix}$

   B to F   rotation $180°$ about $(3\frac{1}{2}, 2)$
   C to E   reflection in the line $x = 6$

5 A to B   reflection in $x = 3$
   C to D   rotation $90°$ about $(8, 4)$

   E to F   translation $\begin{pmatrix} 7 \\ 0 \end{pmatrix}$

6 A to E   reflection in the line $y = 8$
   B to C   rotation $-90°$ about $(2, 4)$

   D to F   translation $\begin{pmatrix} -1 \\ -6 \end{pmatrix}$

7 A to E   translation $\begin{pmatrix} +4 \\ -4 \end{pmatrix}$ *or* reflection in the line $y = x + 3$

   B to D   rotation $180°$ about $(4, 7)$

   C to F   translation $\begin{pmatrix} 8 \\ 6 \end{pmatrix}$

8 A to D   translation $\begin{pmatrix} 5 \\ 2 \end{pmatrix}$

   B to C   reflection in $x = 4$
   E to F   rotation $90°$ about $(9, 4)$

9 A to C   reflection in the line $y = 5$
   B to D   rotation $180°$ about $(3, 6)$

   E to F   translation $\begin{pmatrix} 7 \\ 2 \end{pmatrix}$

Book 3 Unit 4

AT 4/4 (iv)   Pupils construct and interpret simple line graphs.

Exercise 4.1 *page 32*

1 a 10 cm, 50 cm, 65 cm, 95 cm   b 2 p.m. to 3 p.m., 20 cm
   c 8 a.m. to 9 a.m., 5 cm   d 1 p.m. to 2 p.m.
2 a 3000, 6500, 1500, 4500, 9000   b 2 p.m. to 2.30 p.m., 3000

3 a 8 km, 14 km, 6 km, 16 km   **b** 10 a.m. to 10.30 a.m., 5 km
  c 12.30 p.m. to 1.30 p.m.
4 a 30 l, 20 l, 25 l, 15 l **b** 200 km to 300 km, 15 l **c** 55 l
5 a 20 s, 90 s, 100 s, 80 s, 30 s, 10 s   **b** 200 m to 400 m
  c 600 m to 800 m, 50 s
6 a 40, 260, 340, 10, 110   **b** 3 p.m. to 4 p.m., 120
  c 10 a.m. to 11 a.m., 20   **d** £30
7 a 19 l, 8 l, 12 l, 13 l **b** 5 p.m. to 5.30 p.m., 6 l, 30 cups
  c 28 l

Exercise 4.2   *page 36*

1 a £1.20 **b** £2 **c** 20 p **d** 6 kg **e** $2\frac{1}{2}$ kg **f** $4\frac{1}{2}$ kg
2 a 80 p **b** £1.80 **c** £3.40 **d** £2.30 **e** 3 litres **f** 7 litres
  g 13 litres **h** 15.5 litres
3 a £9 **b** £15 **c** £13.50 **d** 10 litres **e** 25 litres **f** 15 litres
4 a £6 **b** £15 **c** £27 **d** 6 m^2 **e** 20 m^2 **f** 14 m^2
5 a £90 **b** £150 **c** £105 **d** 5 m^2 **e** 22.5 m^2 **f** 7.5 m^2
6 a 90 p **b** 75 p **c** £1.05 **d** 15 min **e** 8 min **f** 28 min
7 a £1.80 **b** £1.08 **c** 36 **d** 6
8 a 240 km **b** 200 km **c** 280 km **d** 4 h **e** $1\frac{1}{2}$ h **f** $\frac{1}{2}$ h
9 a 54 km **b** 45 km **c** 42 km **d** 12 km **e** $1\frac{1}{2}$ h **f** $\frac{1}{2}$ h
  g 1 h 20 min   **h** 1 h 40 min
10 a 9 km **b** $7\frac{1}{2}$ km **c** 4 km **d** 45 min **e** 1 h 20 min
  f 20 min

Exercise 4.3   *page 38*

1 a 24 km   **b** 4 km   **c** 7.5 miles   **d** 12.5 miles
2 a 2.5 kg **b** 4 kg **c** 9 kg **d** 16.5 lb **e** 27.5 lb **f** 24.2 lb
3 a 12 litres   **b** 14 litres   **c** 2 litres   **d** 7 pints
  e 17.5 pints   **f** 10.5 pints
4 a 48 litres   **b** 80 litres   **c** 3.5 gallons
5 a S27 **b** S4.50 **c** £6 **d** £10
6 a FF27 **b** FF36 **c** FF63 **d** £6 **e** £8 **f** £9
7 a DM57   **b** DM47.50   **c** £5   **d** £7.50
8 a 60 g **b** 48 g **c** 32 g **d** 11 cm^3 **e** 8 cm^3 **f** 2.5 cm^3
9 a 12 kg **b** 18 kg **c** 6 kg **d** 10 kg **e** 5 litres
  f 17.5 litres   **g** 8 litres   **h** 14 litres
10 a 210 g **b** 245 g **c** 35 g **d** 1 m **e** 1.5 m **f** 2.5 m

Exercise 4.4   *page 39*

1 a Reading, Didcot, Bristol Parkway, Newport
  b 09.15, 10.00, 11.00
2 a Dishforth, Leeming Bar, Durham
  b 10.30, 11.30, 11.45
3 a Sherbrook Valley Head, The Stepping Stones, Shugborough Hall
  b 15.00, 15.30, 15.45
4 a Great Sankey, Rainhill, Liverpool
  b 14.30, 15.15
5 a Stannington, Morpeth, Alnwick, Warrenford, Berwick-on-Tweed
  b 11.15, 11.30, 12.30, 12.45

Exercise 4.5   *page 42*

1 10.00, 10.30, 60 km, 2 h, 70 km h^{-1}
2 13.00, 14.30, 1 h, 3 km h^{-1}
3 09.00, 11.30, 120 km, 60 km h^{-1}
4 11.00, 11.30, 4 h, 64 km h^{-1}
5 120 km h^{-1}, 3 h 30 min, 70 km, 14.30, 15.00, 100 km h^{-1}

Book 3 Unit 5

AT 2/5 (iv)	Pupils calculate fractional or percentage parts of quantities and measuremens, using a calculator where appropriate.
AT 2/6 (ii)	Pupils are aware of which number to consider as 100 per cent, or a whole, in problems involving comparisons, and use this to evaluate one number as a fraction or percentage of another.

Exercise 5.1 *page 44*

1 0.3, 30%	2 0.9, 90%	3 0.1, 10%	4 0.6, 60%
5 0.2, 20%	6 0.14, 14%	7 0.22, 22%	8 0.34, 34%
9 0.58, 58%	10 0.15, 15%	11 0.35, 35%	12 0.05, 5%
13 0.55, 55%	14 0.36, 36%	15 0.48, 48%	16 0.125, 12.5%
17 0.11, 11%	18 0.17, 17%	19 0.47, 47%	20 0.73, 73%
21 0.93, 93%	22 0.87, 87%	23 0.42, 42%	24 0.775, 77.5%
25 0.575, 57.5%			

Exercise 5.2 *page 44*

1 $\frac{3}{100}$, 0.03	2 $\frac{11}{100}$, 0.11	3 $\frac{39}{100}$, 0.39	4 $\frac{53}{100}$, 0.53	5 $\frac{81}{100}$, 0.81
6 $\frac{21}{40}$, 0.42	7 $\frac{19}{50}$, 0.38	8 $\frac{43}{50}$, 0.86	9 $\frac{9}{20}$, 0.45	10 $\frac{13}{20}$, 0.65
11 $\frac{8}{25}$, 0.32	12 $\frac{14}{25}$, 0.56	13 $\frac{1}{25}$, 0.04	14 $\frac{9}{10}$, 0.9	15 $\frac{1}{5}$, 0.2
16 $\frac{9}{50}$, 0.18	17 $\frac{13}{50}$, 0.26	18 $\frac{37}{100}$, 0.37	19 $\frac{41}{100}$, 0.41	20 $\frac{67}{100}$, 0.67
21 $\frac{21}{25}$, 0.84	22 $\frac{20}{25}$, 0.8	23 $\frac{3}{5}$, 0.6	24 $\frac{3}{10}$, 0.3	25 $\frac{1}{10}$, 0.1

Exercise 5.3 *page 44*

1 $\frac{3}{20}$, 15%	2 $\frac{29}{100}$, 29%	3 $\frac{12}{25}$, 48%	4 $\frac{53}{100}$, 53%
5 $\frac{19}{25}$, 76%	6 $\frac{93}{100}$, 93%	7 $\frac{9}{10}$, 90%	8 $\frac{7}{10}$, 70%
9 $\frac{2}{5}$, 40%	10 $\frac{1}{5}$, 20%	11 $\frac{9}{100}$, 9%	12 $\frac{3}{50}$, 6%
13 $\frac{1}{25}$, 4%	14 $\frac{5}{8}$, 62.5%	15 $\frac{23}{40}$, 57.5%	16 $\frac{9}{40}$, 22.5%
17 $\frac{3}{40}$, 7.5%	18 $\frac{3}{200}$, 1.5%	19 $\frac{21}{80}$, 26.25%	20 $\frac{13}{16}$, 81.25%
21 $\frac{7}{16}$, 43.75%	22 $\frac{1}{16}$, 6.25%	23 $\frac{1}{40}$, 2.5%	24 $\frac{1}{100}$, 1%
25 $\frac{1}{1000}$, 0.1%			

Exercise 5.4 *page 44*

1 23	2 33	3 16	4 200	5 8
6 220	7 168	8 46	9 25	10 100
11 100	12 300	13 200	14 300	15 48
16 4.8	17 14	18 7	19 3.5	20 80
21 8	22 0.89	23 17.5	24 32	25 3.2
26 31.5	27 9.6	28 135	29 152.5	30 4444
31 3.6	32 24	33 10	34 1000	35 14
36 1.4	37 60	38 132	39 306	40 275

Exercise 5.5 *page 45*

1 a 72	b 108	c 60	d 20	e 24
2 a 104	b 72	c 182	d 292	e 174
f 405	g 55	h 165	i 95	j 105
3 a 24	b 125	c 70	d 45	e 210
f 93	g 249	h 21	i 57	j 123
4 a 90	b 200	c 232	d 60	e 48
f 96	g 72	h 132	i 36	j 228

Exercise 5.6	*page 46*	**1** £40	**2** £45	**3** 24 g	**4** £36	**5** £12
		6 £54	**7** 15 cm	**8** £48	**9** £88	**10** £10
		11 £9	**12** 15 cm	**13** 28 cm	**14** £24	**15** £21
		16 £48	**17** £21	**18** 36 cm	**19** 18 g	**20** 60 p
		21 72 p	**22** 88 cm	**23** 70 p	**24** £1.50	**25** £1.28
		26 45 p	**27** 90 cm	**28** 750 g	**29** £9	**30** 60 p

Exercise 5.7	*page 47*	**1** 9%	**2** 7%	**3** 8%	**4** 6%	**5** 70%
		6 30%	**7** 90%	**8** 40%	**9** 80%	**10** 60%
		11 40%	**12** 80%	**13** 20%	**14** 35%	**15** 55%
		16 15%	**17** 45%	**18** 75%	**19** 25%	**20** 80%
		21 40%	**22** 60%	**23** 80%	**24** 40%	**25** 80%
		26 60%	**27** 20%	**28** 25%	**29** 75%	**30** $12\frac{1}{2}$%

Exercise 5.8   *page 47*

1 15　**2** 36 min　**3** 27 m^2　**4** 14　　**5** 27　　**6** 4
7 140　**8** 15　　**9** 5, 7, 8　**10** 60, 75, 45, 15, 30　　**11** 30%
12 80%　**13** 70%　**14** 75%　**15** 45%　**16** 75%　**17** 90%
18 80%　**19** 40%, 30%, 10%, 20%　　**20** 6%, 4%, 10%, 8%, 12%

Book 3 Unit 6

AT 3/5 (i)	When constructing models and when drawing or using shapes, pupils measure and draw angles to the nearest degree, and use language ssociated with angle.

Exercise 6.1	*page 49*	**1** 45°	**2** 135°	**3** 180°	**4** 270°	**5** 225°
		6 90°	**7** 45°	**8** 135°	**9** 90°	**10** 135°
		11 270°	**12** 180°	**13** 225°	**14** 45°	**15** 135°
		16 180°	**17** 45°	**18** 225°	**19** 135°	**20** 90°

Exercise 6.2   *page 50*

1 90°　**2** 30°　**3** 120°　**4** 60°　**5** 60°　**6** 180°　**7** 150°　**8** 150°

Exercise 6.3   *page 50*

1 60°	**2** 30°	**3** 90°	**4** 120°	**5** 180°	**6** 90°
7 120°	**8** 150°	**9** 180°	**10** 150°	**11** 270°	**12** 210°

13 30°, 45°, 60°, 90°, 120°, 135°, 180°, 270°
14 30°, 45°, 60°, 90°, 120°, 180°
15 45°, 90°, 180°, 45°, 135°, 90°, 45°

Exercise 6.4	*page 51*	**1** 80°	**2** 60°	**3** 40°	**5** 75°	**5** 55°	**6** 45°
		7 25°	**8** 5°	**9** 78°	**10** 54°	**11** 18°	**12** 24°
		13 $41\frac{1}{2}$°	**14** $7\frac{1}{2}$°	**15** 62.5°	**16** 150°	**17** 140°	**18** 120°
		19 100°	**20** 90°	**21** 10°	**22** 50°	**23** 70°	**24** 175°
		25 165°	**26** 135°	**27** $112\frac{1}{2}$°	**28** 75°	**29** 25°	**30** 82.5°

Exercise 6.5   *page 52*

1 QX̂Y　　　　　　　　　　**2** MX̂Y, LX̂Y
3 LM̂N, MN̂L, ML̂N　　　　　**4** PQ̂R, QP̂R, PR̂S
5 XŴZ, ZX̂Y, XŶZ, XẐY　　**6** PQ̂R, QR̂S, PŜR, SP̂Q
7 MK̂L, KL̂M, KM̂N, KN̂M　**8** XŴZ, WX̂Z, ZX̂Y, WẐX

Exercise 6.6   *page 54*

1 a 10°, 20°, 30°, 50°, 80°   b 90°, 100°, 110°, 120°, 140°
  c 150°, 170°, 180°, 5°, 15°   d 35°, 65°, 75°, 85°, 105°
  e 115°, 125°, 145°, 165°, 10° f 30°, 40°, 60°, 70°, 80°
  g 90°, 100°, 130°, 150°, 160° h 170°, 180°, 15°, 35°, 55°
  i 65°, 75°, 95°, 105°, 115°   j 145°, 165°, 175°
2 a 4°, 7°, 13°, 18°, 22°   b 26°, 31°, 44°, 57°, 69°
  c 74°, 86°, 93°, 108°, 114°   d 127°, 134°, 148°, 157°, 162°
  e 171°, 177°, 3°, 9°, 18°   f 23°, 32°, 46°, 53°, 66°
  g 72°, 87°, 94°, 106°, 111°   h 123°, 136°, 149°, 154°, 158°
  i 162°, 167°, 173°, 176°

Exercise 6.7   *page 55*

1 30°   2 50°   3 55°   4 75°   5 25°
6 60°   7 70°   8 40°   9 45°   10 35°
11 140°   12 130°   13 135°   14 145°   15 105°
16 120°   17 100°   18 160°   19 165°   20 125°
21 50°   22 60°, 30°   23 45°, 45°   24 135°   25 60°, 120°
26 135°, 90°

Exercise 6.9   *page 61*

1 80°   2 70°   3 90°   4 30°   5 80°
6 60°   7 110°   8 100°   9 30°   10 50°

Exercise 6.10   *page 62*

1 050°   2 080°   3 120°   4 160°   5 220°   6 250°   7 230°
8 260°   9 190°   10 180°   11 320°   12 350°   13 330°   14 290°
15 270°   16 300°

Exercise 6.12   *page 64*

1 20 m, 150°   2 70 m, 135°   3 70 km, 045°
4 175 km, 060°   5 200 km, 240°   6 10 m, 240°

Exercise 6.13   *page 65*

1 50°   2 75°   3 45°   4 125°   5 95°
6 70°   7 80°   8 110°   9 70°   10 20°

Exercise 6.14   *page 65*

1 60°   2 120°   3 120°   4 110°   5 70°   6 60°

Exercise 6.15   *page 66*

1 120°, 60°, 120°   2 110°, 70°, 110°   3 160°, 20°, 160°
4 105°, 75°, 105°   5 155°, 25°, 155°   6 80°, 100°, 80°
7 50°, 130°, 50°   8 30°, 150°, 30°   9 40°, 140°, 40°
10 45°, 135°, 45°

Exercise 6.16   *page 67*

1 80°, acute-angled   2 50°, acute-angled   3 70°, acute-angled
4 20°, acute-angled   5 60°, right-angled   6 90°, right-angled
7 90°, right-angled   8 40°, obtuse-angled   9 100°, obtuse-angled
10 120°, obtuse-angled

Exercise 6.17   *page 67*

1 60°, 120°   2 50°, 130°   3 90°, 90°
4 100°, 80°   5 110°, 70°   6 80°, 100°
7 120°, 60°   8 60°, 120°, 60°, 120°   9 40°, 140°, 40°, 140°
10 130°, 50°, 130°, 50°   11 70°, 80°   12 50°, 70°
13 60°, 100°   14 100°, 50°   15 90°, 50°
16 110°, 70°, 90°   17 50°, 130°, 20°   18 80°, 40°
19 50°, 50°   20 110°, 40°   21 90°, 60°
22 100°, 80°, 30°   23 40°, 140°, 20°   24 110°, 70°, 20°

Book 3   Unit 7

AT 4/4 (v)   Pupils understand and use simple vocabulary associated with probability, including 'fair', 'certain' and 'likely'.

AT 4/5 (v)   Pupils find and justify probabilities, and approximations to these, selecting and using methods based on equally likely outcomes and experimental evidence, as appropriate. They understand that different outcomes may result from repeating an experiment.

Exercise 7.1   *page 69*

Many of these questions will provide debate about the general meaning of 'fair' and the mathematical meaning.

1 **a** fair   **b** not fair   **c** not fair
   d could be fair – there can be leaves on pear tree April/May – Sept/Oct.
   e fair   **f** not fair   **g** not fair
   h fair – who chooses first? Some colours are more common than others.

2 **a** not fair   **b** fair
   c fair – if they both have good eyesight and same amount of window, etc.
   d not fair – not the same questions   **e** not fair
   f fair – if they don't try to attract his attention   **g** fair
   h fair – if neither has any knowledge of how many 10 p coins are in her pocket

3 **a** fair   **b** fair   **c** not fair
   d fair – if no-one has prior knowledge of garden   **e** unfair
   f fair

4 **a** not fair   **b** fair   **c** not fair   **d** fair
   e not fair   **f** not fair – pupils numbered 1–4 cannot be selected
   g fair   **h** not fair

5 **a** fair (if no wind, etc.)   **b** not fair   **c** fair
   d not fair   **e** fair   **f** fair
   g fair – if whoever wins has no preferences

Exercise 7.2   *page 71*

1 **a** $\frac{3}{7}$ **b** $\frac{2}{7}$ 2 **a** $\frac{1}{2}$ **b** $\frac{1}{3}$

3 **a** $\frac{1}{3}$ **b** $\frac{1}{3}$ **c** $\frac{1}{2}$ **d** $\frac{1}{2}$

4 **a** $\frac{3}{8}$ **b** $\frac{1}{4}$ **c** $\frac{1}{2}$ **d** $\frac{1}{2}$

5 **a** $\frac{3}{8}$ **b** $\frac{1}{4}$ **c** $\frac{5}{8}$ 6 **a** $\frac{3}{10}$ **b** $\frac{2}{5}$ **c** $\frac{3}{5}$

7 **a** $\frac{3}{4}$ **b** $\frac{1}{4}$ 8 **a** $\frac{3}{5}$ **b** $\frac{2}{5}$

9 **a** $\frac{5}{6}$ **b** $\frac{1}{6}$ 10 **a** $\frac{1}{2}$ **b** $\frac{3}{10}$ **c** $\frac{1}{5}$

Exercise 7.3   *page 72*

1 **a** $\frac{18}{30} = \frac{9}{15} = 0.6 = 60\%$ **b** $\frac{10}{30} = \frac{1}{3} = 0.333 = 33.3\%$

   c $\frac{2}{30} = \frac{1}{15} = 0.066 = 6.6\%$

2 **a** $\frac{6}{24} = \frac{1}{4} = 0.25 = 25\%$ **b** $\frac{4}{24} = \frac{1}{6} = 0.167 = 16.7\%$

   c $\frac{6}{24} = \frac{1}{4} = 0.25 = 25\%$ **d** $\frac{8}{24} = \frac{1}{3} = 0.333 = 33.3\%$

   e $\frac{10}{24} = \frac{5}{12} = 0.417 = 41.7\%$ **f** $\frac{14}{24} = \frac{7}{12} = 0.583 = 58.3\%$

3 **a** $\frac{8}{20} = \frac{2}{5} = 0.4 = 40\%$ **b** $\frac{5}{20} = \frac{1}{4} = 0.25 = 25\%$

   c $\frac{3}{20} = 0.15 = 15\%$ **d** $\frac{4}{20} = \frac{1}{5} = 0.2 = 20\%$

   e $\frac{12}{20} = \frac{3}{5} = 0.6 = 60\%$

4 **a** $\frac{1}{6} = 0.167 = 16.7\%$ **b** $\frac{3}{6} = \frac{1}{2} = 0.5 = 50\%$

   c $\frac{3}{6} = \frac{1}{2} = 0.5 = 50\%$ **d** $\frac{2}{6} = \frac{1}{3} = 0.333 = 33.3\%$

  e $\frac{3}{6} = \frac{1}{2} = 0.5 = 50\%$ **f** $\frac{2}{6} = \frac{1}{3} = 0.333 = 33.3\%$

  g $\frac{3}{6} = \frac{1}{2} = 0.5 = 50\%$

5 a $\frac{5}{12} = 0.417 = 41.7\%$ **b** $\frac{3}{12} = \frac{1}{4} = 0.25 = 25\%$

  c $\frac{4}{12} = \frac{1}{3} = 0.333 = 33.3\%$ **d** $\frac{4}{12} = \frac{1}{3} = 0.333 = 33.3\%$

  e $\frac{2}{12} = \frac{1}{6} = 0.167 = 16.7\%$

6 a $\frac{3}{12} = \frac{1}{4} = 0.25 = 25\%$ **b** $\frac{9}{12} = \frac{3}{4} = 0.75 = 75\%$

  c $\frac{4}{12} = \frac{1}{3} = 0.333 = 33.3\%$ **d** $\frac{6}{12} = \frac{1}{2} = 0.5 = 50\%$

7 a $\frac{3}{12} = \frac{1}{4} = 0.25 = 25\%$ **b** $\frac{2}{12} = \frac{1}{6} = 0.167 = 16.7\%$

  c $\frac{2}{12} = \frac{1}{6} = 0.167 = 16.7\%$ **d** $\frac{4}{12} = \frac{1}{3} = 0.333 = 33.3\%$

  e $\frac{4}{12} = \frac{1}{3} = 0.333 = 33.3\%$ **f** $\frac{4}{12} = \frac{1}{3} = 0.333 = 33.3\%$

  g $\frac{7}{12} = 0.583 = 58.3\%$

8 a $\frac{3}{8} = 0.375 = 37.5\%$ **b** $\frac{5}{8} = 0.625 = 62.5\%$

  c $\frac{2}{8} = \frac{1}{4} = 0.25 = 25\%$ **d** $\frac{3}{8} = 0.375 = 37.5\%$

  e $\frac{5}{8} = 0.625 = 62.5\%$ **f** $\frac{1}{8} = 0.125 = 12.5\%$

9 a $\frac{8}{40} = \frac{1}{5} = 0.2 = 20\%$ **b** $\frac{12}{40} = \frac{3}{10} = 0.3 = 30\%$

  c $\frac{4}{40} = \frac{1}{10} = 0.1 = 10\%$ **d** $\frac{16}{40} = \frac{2}{5} = 0.4 = 40\%$

  e $\frac{20}{40} = \frac{1}{2} = 0.5 = 50\%$ **f** $\frac{12}{40} = \frac{3}{10} = 0.3 = 30\%$

  g $\frac{24}{40} = \frac{3}{5} = 0.6 = 60\%$

10 a $\frac{4}{52} = \frac{1}{13} = 0.077 = 7.7\%$ **b** $\frac{12}{52} = \frac{3}{13} = 0.231 = 23.1\%$

  c $\frac{36}{52} = \frac{9}{13} = 0.692 = 69.2\%$ **d** $\frac{20}{52} = \frac{5}{13} = 0.385 = 38.5\%$

  e $\frac{16}{52} = \frac{4}{13} = 0.308 = 30.8\%$

Exercise 7.4 *page 74*   **1** $\frac{1}{4}$ **2** $\frac{1}{4}$ **3** $\frac{3}{10}$ **4** $\frac{1}{4}$ **5** $\frac{1}{49}$ **6** 0.1

  7 0.05   **8** 0.56   **9** 0.67   **10** 0.2   **11** 75%   **12** 40%

  13 37.5%   **14** 71.4%   **15** 6.25%   **16** 55%

Exercise 7.5 *page 76*   **1 b** experiment   **2 c** experiment   **3 b** check records

  4 b check records   **5 b** survey   **6 b** check records or survey

  7 b check records   **8 b** check records   **9 b** experiment

  10 b experiment

Book 3 Unit 8

AT 4/5 (ii)	Pupils interpret graphs and diagrams, including pie charts, and draw conclusions.
AT 4/5 (ii)	Pupils compare two simple distributions, using the range and one of the measures of average.
AT 4/6 (iii)	Pupils construct pie charts.

Exercise 8.1 *page 78*   **1** 80, 60, 50, 30, 20   **2** 60, 50, 40, 30

  9 (1) 8   (2) 5   (3) 3   (4) 6   (5) 4   (6) 4

Exercise 8.2 *page 81*   **1** mode   = 57 s   **2** mode   = 43 kg

  median = 57 s   median = 43 kg

  range = 4 s   range = 6 kg

3 mode   = 4
median = 3
range   = 6

4 mode   = 3
median = 3
range   = 5

5 mode   = 3
median = 3
range   = 4

Exercise 8.3   *page 83*   **1** 1.6   **2** 5.45 or 5th   **3** 6.8   **4** 32.8 min   **5** 1.9

Exercise 8.4   *page 84*

1 mode   = 4
median = 4
mean   = 4.6
range   = 10

2 mode   = 50
median = 50
mean   = 51
range   = 80

3 b

no. of bottles per household	1	2	3	4	5	6
frequency	6	10	11	8	3	2

c mode   = 3
median = 3
mean   = 2.95
range   = 5

4 a

caps	1	2	3	4	5	6
frequency	1	3	5	3	2	1

b mode   = 3
median = 3
mean   = 3.3
range   = 5

5 a

temperature	$0°$	$1°$	$2°$	$3°$	$4°$	$5°$	$6°$
frequency	2	3	3	5	8	6	4

b mode   = 4 °C
median = 4 °C
mean   = 3.5 °C
range   = 6 °C

Exercise 8.5   *page 87*

1 a School M   mode   = 1
median = 1
mean   = 1.78
range   = 4

School N   mode   = 1
median = 2
mean   = 2.74
range   = 3

2 a Group A   mode   = 2
median = 2
mean   = 2.44
range   = 8

Group B   mode   = 6
median = 6
mean   = 5.63
range   = 10

3 a Striko   mode   = 40
median = 40
mean   = 40.4
range   = 8

Katchwell   mode   = 39
median = 39
mean   = 39.4
range   = 3

Book 4 Unit 1

AT 2/6 (iv)   Pupils calculate using ratio in appropriate situations.

Exercise 1.1 *page 1*

1 4:5	**2** 5:6	**3** 3:8	**4** 5:8	**5** 1:2	**6** 3:4
7 4:5	**8** 5:8	**9** 9:10	**10** 1:3	**11** 2:3	**12** 4:5
13 9:10	**14** 2:3	**15** 3:4	**16** 2:5	**17** 5:8	**18** 1:5
19 3:5	**20** 5:6	**21** 5:8	**22** 3:5	**23** 7:8	**24** 2:3
25 4:5	**26** 3:4	**27** 3:5	**28** 2:5	**29** 5:8	**30** 1:5
31 1:4	**32** 1:6	**33** 2:5	**34** 3:10	**35** 1:4	**36** 4:5
37 4:5	**38** 3:4	**39** 3:5	**40** 3:8	**41** 1:2	**42** 3:10
43 1:6	**44** 9:10	**45** 4:5	**46** 3:4	**47** 5:6	**48** 1:4
49 1:8	**50** 1:5				

Exercise 1.2 *page 1*

1 2:3	**2** 7:10	**3** 4:5	**4** 3:4	**5** 3:5
6 4:5	**7** 2:3	**8** 1:3	**9** 1:4	**10** 3:4

Exercise 1.3 *page 2*

1 £32, £16   **2** £45, £15   **3** £64, £16
4 £78, £13   **5** £42, £28   **6** £75, £45
7 64 ml, 48 ml   **8** 72 ml, 90 ml   **9** 75 g, 125 g
10 36 g, 84 g   **11** £54, £36, £18   **12** £80, £48, £16
13 £60, £45, £30   **14** £90, £75, £15   **15** £120, £100, £80
16 180 g, 90 g, 45 g   **17** 120 kg, 150 kg, 180 kg
18 300 ml, 450 ml, 750 ml   **19** 120 ml, 200 ml, 240 ml   **20** 12, 18 and 20

Exercise 1.4 *page 3*

1 45 p   **2** 40 p   **3 a** 45 p   **b** 81 p
4 a £28   **b** £40   **5 a** £32   **b** £52   **6 a** £15   **b** £25
7 a £15   **b** £21   **8 a** 30 p   **b** 45 p   **c** £1
9 36 p   **10** 150 cm   **11** 60 kg
12 a 250 ml   **b** 400 ml   **13 a** 14   **b** 26   **14 a** 55 cm   **b** 1 m
15 a 150 g   **b** 200 g   **c** 450 g   **16 a** 10   **b** 16   **c** 30
17 a 8   **b** 14   **c** 28   **18** 18 p   **19 a** £8   **b** £36
20 8 years

Exercise 1.5 *page 5*

1 54 p   **2** 64 p   **3** £4.50
4 a 81 min   **b** 36 min   **5 a** £25   **b** £40   **6** 96 p
7 £2.70   **8 a** £1.28   **b** £1.60   **9 a** £1.08   **b** £1.44
10 a £7.20   **b** £19.20   **11 a** £11.20   **b** £33.60   **12 a** £1.50   **b** £3.50
13 a £3.60   **b** £9.60   **c** £14.40   **14 a** £22.50   **b** £30   **c** £90
15 a £4.00   **b** £6.00   **c** £15.00   **16** 5   **17** 3
18 15   **19 a** 3   **b** 8   **20 a** 2   **b** 7
21 a 2   **b** 5   **22 a** 4   **b** 10   **23 a** 5   **b** 8
24 a 25   **b** 45   **25 a** 3   **b** 10   **26 a** 3   **b** 7
27 a 4   **b** 7   **c** 9   **28 a** 3   **b** 8   **c** 14   **29 a** 15   **b** 50
30 a 8   **b** 20

Book 4 Unit 2

AT 3/6 (ii)   Pupils know and use the properties of quadrilaterals in classifying different types of quadrilateral. They solve problems using angle and symmetry properties of polygons and proprties of intersecting and parallel lines, and explain these properties.

Exercise 2.1 *page 7*

1 $\hat{b}, \hat{c}, \hat{y}, \hat{z}$ 2 $\hat{m}, \hat{n}, \hat{q}, \hat{r}$ 3 $\hat{c}, \hat{d}, \hat{u}, \hat{v}$ 4 $\hat{r}, \hat{q}, \hat{z}, \hat{y}$
5 $\hat{c}, \hat{b}, \hat{y}, \hat{z}$ 6 $\hat{m}, \hat{n}, \hat{r}, \hat{q}$

Exercise 2.2 *page 8*

1 $\hat{c}, \hat{d}$ 2 $\hat{r}, \hat{s}$ 3 $\hat{m}, \hat{n}$ 4 $\hat{x}, \hat{y}$ 5 $\hat{p}, \hat{q}$ 6 $\hat{s}, \hat{r}$

Exercise 2.3 *page 8*

1 130°	2 120°	3 110°, 70°	4 140°, 140°
5 80°, 80°	6 60°	7 110°	8 80°
9 70°	10 50°	11 60°, 120°	12 110°, 70°, 110°
13 150°, 30°, 30°	14 40°, 140°, 140°	15 50°, 50°, 130°	16 120°, 120°, 60°

Exercise 2.4 *page 9*

1 $\hat{p}, \hat{q}$ 2 $\hat{x}, \hat{y}$ 3 $\hat{v}, \hat{u}$ 4 $\hat{s}, \hat{r}$ 5 $\hat{x}, \hat{y}$ 6 $\hat{u}, \hat{y}$

Exercise 2.5 *page 10*

1 60°	2 130°	3 40°	4 110°
5 80°	6 60°, 60°	7 140°, 140°	8 50°, 130°
9 70°, 110°	10 120°, 60°	11 50°, 50°	12 140°, 140°, 40°
13 110°, 110°, 70°	14 120°, 120°		15 120°, 120°, 120°
16 130°, 50°			

Exercise 2.6 *page 10*

1 $\hat{x}, \hat{y}$ 2 $\hat{r}, \hat{s}$ 3 $\hat{z}, \hat{y}$ 4 $\hat{y}, \hat{x}$ 5 $\hat{u}, \hat{v}$ 6 $\hat{p}, \hat{q}$

Exercise 2.7 *page 11*

1 120°	2 50°	3 110°	4 40°
5 100°, 80°	6 60°, 120°	7 130°, 130°	8 70°, 70°
9 140°, 40°	10 80°, 100°	11 50°, 130°	12 110°, 70°
13 60°, 120°, 60°	14 130°, 50°, 130°	15 70°, 110°, 110°	
16 140°, 40°, 40°	17 60°, 120°, 120°	18 100°, 80°, 80°	

Exercise 2.8 *page 13*

1 B	2 C	3 E	4 F	5 G	6 D	7 A	8 C
9 B	10 E	11 G	12 F	13 B	14 C	15 G	

Exercise 2.9 *page 14*

1 50°, 80°	2 65°, 50°	3 35°, 110°	4 32°, 116°
5 55°, 55°	6 72°, 72°	7 25°, 25°	8 36°, 36°
9 150°, 75°, 75°	10 124°, 62°, 62°	11 40°, 70°, 70°	12 76°, 52°, 52°
13 66°, 48°, 132°	14 48°, 84°, 96°	15 75°, 30°, 150°	16 54°, 72°, 108°

Exercise 2.10 *page 14*

1 50°	2 110°	3 60°	4 125°
5 40°, 80°, 60°	6 30°, 80°, 80°	7 50°, 60°, 70°	
8 55°, 55°, 45°	9 45°, 65°, 65°	10 45°, 60°, 75°	
11 35°, 35°, 95°	12 70°, 55°, 55°	13 70°, 70°, 70°, 70°	
14 40°, 40°, 40°, 40°	15 45°, 90°, 45°, 90°	16 45°, 45°, 90°, 90°	

Exercise 2.11   *page 15*

1 55°, 95°, 30°, 150°	**2** 65°, 25°, 90°
3 75°, 75°, 75°, 75°, 30°	**4** 45°, 135°, 45°, 45°
5 90°, 90°, 60°, 30°	**6** 105°, 75°, 120°, 60°, 45°
7 95°, 85°, 85°, 140°, 40°, 55°	**8** 65°, 65°, 115°, 65°, 65°, 50°
9 30°, 30°, 90°, 90°, 90°	**10** 30°, 60°, 60°
11 80°, 60°, 60°, 40°	**12** 25°, 130°, 130°, 25°, 155°

Exercise 2.12   *page 16*

	square	rectangle	rhombus	parallelogram	kite	isosceles trapezium
1	Y	N	Y	N	N	N
2	Y	Y	Y	Y	N	One pair are
3	Y	N	Y	N	Y	N
4	Y	Y	Y	Y	N	One pair are
5	Y	Y	N	N	N	N
6	Y	Y	Y	Y	N	N
7	Y	Y	N	N	N	Y
8	Y	N	Y	N	Y	N
9	Y	Y	Y	Y	Y	Y
a	2	2	2	0	1	1
b	4	2	2	2	0	0

Exercise 2.15   *page 19*

1 a 5	**b** 8	**c** 9	**d** 10	**e** 12
2 a 2, 3	**b** 5, 6	**c** 6, 7	**d** 7, 8	**e** 9, 10
3 a 540°	**b** 1080°	**c** 1260°	**d** 1440°	**e** 1800°
4 a 108°	**b** 135°	**c** 140°	**d** 144°	**e** 150°

Exercise 2.16   *page 19*

1 a 5	**b** 6	**c** 9	**d** 10	**e** 12

2 360° in all cases

3 a 72°	**b** 60°	**c** 40°	**d** 36°	**e** 30°

4 180° in all cases

Exercise 2.17   *page 20*

1 isosceles triangle, isosceles trapezium
2 isosceles triangle, kite, kite
3 square, rectangle, kite, isosceles trapezium, isosceles triangle (right-angled), isosceles triangle (right-angled), isosceles triangle
4 isosceles triangle, isosceles trapezium, isosceles trapezium
5 regular nonagon, equilateral triangle, isosceles trapezium
6 regular pentagon, regular pentagon, rhombus, isosceles trapezium, kite
7 regular hexagon, equilateral triangle, rhombus, isosceles trapezium
8 square, regular octagon

Exercise 2.19   *page 23*

1 ADM and BCN
2 ACX and ABX
3 BPQ and DSR
4 ABF and DCE, BCF and ECF
5 AWZ and CYX, BWX and DYZ
6 AKN and BKL, DMN and CML

7 AED and ABC, ADM and ACM
8 ADE and CDE, ADB and CDB, AEB and CEB
9 ABC and EFG, ACH and EGD, CHD and GDH
10 AXC and BXD, ABC and ABD, ACD and BCD

Exercise 2.20   *page 24*

1 **a** regular hexagon   **b** 120°, 60°, 60°   **c** 360°
2 **a** regular pentagon   **b** 108°, 72°, 36°   **c** 180°
3 160°, 40°   4 110°, 110°, 40°

Book 4   Unit 3

AT 2/6 (v)	When exploring number patterns, pupils find and describe in words the rule for the next term or *n*th term of a sequence where the rule is linear.
AT 2/7 (v)	Pupils find and describe in symbols the next term or *n*th term of a sequence where the rule is quadratic.

Exercise 3.1   *page 26*

1 Each term is the one before it plus 2: 9, 11
2 Each term is twice the one before it: 16, 32
3 Each term is the one before it plus 0.2: 2.0, 2.2
4 Each term is 4 times the one before it: 256, 1024
5 Each term is 13 more than the one before it: 59, 72
6 Each term is the sum of the two previous terms: 13, 21
7 Each term is the product of the two previous terms: 256, 8192
8 Each term is 5 times the one before it: 625, 3125
9 Each term is 5 times the one before it: 62.5, 312.5
10 Each term is 50 less than the one before it: 0, −50
11 Each term is half the one before it: 62.5, 31.25
12 Each term is half the one before it: 6.25, 3.125
13 Each term is 300 less than the one before it: −200, −500
14 Each term is a quarter of the one before it: 0.125, 0.03125
15 Each term is 10 times the one before it: 10 000, 100 000
16 Each term is 11 more than the one before it: 65, 76
17 Each term is 2 times the one before it, plus 1: 31, 63
18 Each term is 3 times the one before it, plus 1: 121, 364
19 Each term is 3 times the one before it, minus 1: 41, 122
20 Each term is 5 times the one before it, minus 3: 157, 782

Exercise 3.2   *page 26*

1 1, 3, 9, 27, 81   2 6, 11, 16, 21, 26
3 2, 6, 18, 54, 162   4 100, 95, 90, 85, 80
5 4000, 1000, 250, 62.5, 15.625   6 1, 7, 19, 43, 91
7 4, 7, 13, 25, 49   8 1, 7, 31, 127, 511
9 1000, 210, 52, 20.4, 14.08   10 1, 20, 210, 2110, 21 110

Exercise 3.3   *page 27*

1 Multiplied by 3: 15, 18   2 Multiplied by 3, minus 1: 14, 17
3 Minus 6: −1, 0   4 Multiplied by 4: 20, 24
5 Multiplied by 4, plus 1: 21, 25   6 Multiplied by 4, plus 2: 22, 26
7 Multiplied by 4, minus 1: 19, 23   8 Multiplied by 4, minus 2: 18, 22
9 Multiplied by 5: 25, 30   10 Multiplied by 5, plus 1: 26, 31
11 Multiplied by 5, plus 2: 27, 32   12 Multiplied by 5, plus 3: 28, 33
13 Multiplied by 5, minus 1: 24, 29   14 Multiplied by 5, minus 5: 20, 25
15 Multiplied by 5, minus 6: 19, 24   16 Multiplied by 6, minus 1: 29, 35

17 Multiplied by 6, plus 1: 31, 37   **18** Multiplied by 10, plus 3: 53, 63
19 Multiplied by 10, minus 3: 47, 57   **20** Divided by 10: 0.5, 0.6

Exercise 3.4   *page 27*

1 7, 14, 21, 28, 35; 70   **2** 12, 13, 14, 15, 16; 21
3 −4, −3, −2, −1, 0; 5   **4** 0.5, 1, 1.5, 2, 2.5; 5
5 13, 15, 17, 19, 21; 31   **6** 24, 26, 28, 30, 32; 42
7 6, 13, 20, 27, 34; 69   **8** 0, 7, 14, 21, 28; 63
9 5.5, 6, 6.5, 7, 7.5; 10   **10** 3, 3.5, 4, 4.5, 5; 7.5
11 −3.75, −3.5, −3.25, −3, −2.75; −1.5
12 −0.75, −0.5, −0.25, 0, 0.25; 1.5
13 7, 12, 17, 22, 27; 52   **14** 15, 20, 25, 30, 35; 60
15 15, 18, 21, 24, 27; 42   **16** 39, 42, 45, 48, 51; 66
17 2, 3.5, 5, 6.5, 8; 15.5   **18** 2.25, 3.75, 5.25, 6.75, 8.25; 15.75
19 −1, 0.5, 0, 0.5, 1; 3.5   **20** −0.25, 0.25, 0.75, 1.25, 1.75; 4.25

Exercise 3.5   *page 28*

1 $T_{n+1} = T_n + 7$ **2** $T_{n+1} = 2T_n$
3 $T_{n+1} = T_n + 4$ **4** $T_{n+1} = 3T_n$
5 $T_{n+1} = T_n + 2$ **6** $T_{n+1} = 7T_n$
7 $T_{n+1} = T_n - 2$ **8** $T_{n+1} = T_n \div 2$
9 $T_{n+1} = T_n - 10$ **10** $T_{n+1} = T_n \div 10$
11 $T_{n+1} = 2T_n$ **12** $T_{n+1} = 2T_n + 1$
13 $T_{n+1} = 2T_n + 3$ **14** $T_{n+1} = 2T_n + 4$
15 $T_{n+1} = 3T_n$ **16** $T_{n+1} = 3T_n + 1$
17 $T_{n+1} = 3T_n + 2$ **18** $T_{n+1} = 3T_n - 1$
19 $T_{n+1} = 4T_n$ **20** $T_{n+1} = 4T_n - 2$

Exercise 3.6   *page 28*

1 1, 14, 27, 40, 53   **2** 1, 5, 9, 13, 17
3 1, 6, 36, 216, 1296   **4** 1, 8, 64, 512, 4096
5 20, 15, 10, 5, 0   **6** 12, 11, 10, 9, 8
7 1000, 100, 10, 1, 0.1   **8** 512, 256, 128, 64, 32
9 1, 8, 22, 50, 106   **10** 1, 8, 50, 302, 1814
11 1, 2, 7, 32, 157   **12** 1, 6, 41, 286, 2001
13 260, 132, 68, 36, 20   **14** 11 725, 2350, 475, 100, 25
15 603, 198, 63, 18, 3   **16** 1956, 484, 116, 24, 1
17 1, 16, 61, 196, 601   **18** 1, 8, 57, 400, 2801
19 1, 20, 210, 2110, 21 110   **20** 1, 1, 1, 1, 1

Exercise 3.7   *page 29*

1 $T_n = 3n$ **2** $T_n = 4n$ **3** $T_n = 5n$ **4** $T_n = 6n$
5 $T_n = 9n$ **6** $T_n = n + 8$ **7** $T_n = n + 6$ **8** $T_n = n + 100$
9 $T_n = n - 6$ **10** $T_n = n - 11$ **11** $T_n = \frac{n}{2}$ **12** $T_n = \frac{n}{4}$
13 $T_n = \frac{n}{100}$ **14** $T_n = \frac{n}{8}$ **15** $T_n = \frac{n}{5}$ **16** $T_n = 2n + 1$
17 $T_n = 3n + 3$ **18** $T_n = 10n + 1$ **19** $T_n = 10n + 10$ **20** $T_n = 2n + 2$

Exercise 3.8   *page 29*

1 9, 14, 19, 24, 29; 54
2 1, 6, 11, 16, 21; 46
3 9, 13, 17, 21, 25; 45
4 −1, 3, 7, 11, 15; 35
5 1.25, 2.5, 3.75, 5, 6.25; 12.5
6 0.8, 1.6, 2.4, 3.2, 4; 8
7 5.25, 5.5, 5.75, 6, 6.25; 7.5
8 4.2, 4.4, 4.6, 4.8, 5; 6
9 −4.75, −4.5, −4.25, −4, −3.75; −2.5
10 −3.8, −3.6, −3.4, −3.2, −3.0; −2
11 1, 1.2, 1.4, 1.6, 1.8; 2.8

12 1. 5, 1.75, 2, 2.25, 2.5; 3.75
13 −0.6, −0.4, −0.2, 0, 0.2; 1.2
14 −1, −0.75, −0.5, −0.25, 0; 1.25
15 −15, −10, −5, 0, 5; 30
16 −16, −12, −8, −4, 0; 20

Exercise 3.9   *page 30*

1 $T_n = 5 \times 2^{(n-1)}$ **2** $T_n = 6 \times 2^{(n-1)}$
3 $T_n = 7 \times 2^{(n-1)}$ **4** $T_n = 10 \times 2^{(n-1)}$
5 $T_n = 8 \times 2^{(n-1)}$ **6** $T_n = 2^n$
7 $T_n = 2 \times 3^{(n-1)}$ **8** $T_n = 3^{(n-1)}$
9 $T_n = 2^{(n-1)}$ **10** $T_n = 10^{(n-1)}$
11 $T_n = 2 \times 5^{(n-1)}$ **12** $T_n = 7 \times 11^{(n-1)}$
13 $T_n = 4^n$ **14** $T_n = 9^{(n-1)}$
15 $T_n = 3 \times 9^{(n-1)}$ **16** $T_n = 6^{(n-1)}$
17 $T_n = 8^{(n-1)}$ **18** $T_n = 5 \times 8^{(n-1)}$
19 $T_n = 2 \times 8^{(n-1)}$ **20** $T_n = 3^n$

Exercise 3.10   *page 30*

1 5, 30, 180, 1080; 50 388 480
2 4, 28, 196, 1372; 161 414 428
3 7, 28, 112, 448; 1 835 008
4 8, 24, 72, 216; 157 464
5 3, 24, 192, 1536; 402 653 184
6 2, 14, 98, 686; 80 707 214
7 7, 14, 28, 56; 3584
8 1, 4, 16, 64; 262 144
9 4, 16, 64, 256; 1 048 576
10 3, 30, 300, 3000; 3 000 000 000
11 10, 30, 90, 270; 196 830
12 1, 3, 9, 27; 19 683
13 10, 100, 1000, 10 000; 10 000 000 000
14 15, 45, 135, 405; 295 245
15 15, 75, 375, 1875; 29 296 875
16 3, 15, 75, 375; 5 859 375

Exercise 3.11   *page 31*

1 **a** $T_n = 2n + 2$, 22 marigolds   **b** $T_n = 2n + 8$, 28 marigolds
   c $T_n = 2n + 10$, 30 marigolds
2 **a** $T_n = 3n + 20$ **b** $T_n = n + 20$
   c $T_n = 2n + 20$ **d** $T_n = 5n + 20$
   e $T_n = 10n + 20$
3 **a** $T_n = 1000 - 5n$ **b** $T_n = 1000 - 3n$
   c $T_n = 1000 - 7n$ **d** $T_n = 1000 - 10n$
   e $T_n = 1000 - 14n$
4 **a** $T_n = 400 - 10n$ **b** $T_n = 400 - 20n$
   c $T_n = 400 - 5n$ **d** $T_n = 400 - 17n$
   e $T_n = 400 - 25n$
5 **a** $T_n = 10 \times 2^n$ **b** £102.40
6 **a** $T_n = 2^{(n-1)}$ **b** 524 288   **c** 9.22×10^{18} **d** The kingdom
7 **a** $T_n = 25\,000 \times (1.1)^n$

   b

end of year	population
1	27 500
2	30 250
3	33 275
4	36 603

After 4 years

	c *end of year*	*pop. Gastropoll*	*pop. Strovney*
	1	27 500	24 000
	2	30 250	28 000
	3	33 275	34 560

After 3 years

8 a $T_n = 24 \times 3^n$ **b** 8   **c** 1 417 176

	d *end of year*	*no. rabbits*
	1	72
	2	216
	3	648
	4	1944
	5	5832

Exercise 3.12 *page 32*

1	2, 8, 18, 32, 50	**2**	3, 12, 27, 48, 75
3	5, 20, 45, 80, 125	**4**	2, 5, 10, 17, 26
5	0, 3, 8, 15, 24	**6**	3, 6, 11, 18, 27
7	−1, 2, 7, 14, 23	**8**	0, 2, 6, 12, 20
9	3, 9, 19, 33, 51	**10**	3, 10, 21, 36, 55
11	3, 7, 13, 21, 31	**12**	7, 11, 17, 25, 35
13	5, 12, 23, 38, 57	**14**	6, 14, 26, 42, 62
15	1, 6, 15, 28, 45	**16**	0, 4, 12, 24, 40
17	6, 11, 20, 33, 50	**18**	4, 5, 8, 13, 20
19	−1, −1, −4, 5, 11	**20**	5, 13, 27, 47, 73

Exercise 3.13 *page 33*

1 b 12×13 **c** 100×101 **d** $n \times (n + 1)$ **e** $T_n = \dfrac{n(n + 1)}{2}$

2 a 6   **b** 12   **c** 20   **d** $T_n = n(n - 1)$

3 a 924   **b** $2n(n - 1)$

4 a 1   **b** 6   **c** 12   **d** 8

   e 27 painted on 0 faces   **f** $(n - 2)^2$, $6(n - 2)^2$, $12(n - 2)$, 8
   54 painted on 1 face
   36 painted on 2 faces
   8 painted on 3 faces

Book 4 Unit 4

AT 3/6 (iv)	Pupils understand and use appropriate formulae for finding the areas of plane rectilinear figures.

Exercise 4.1 *page 34*

1	300 cm², 74 cm	**2**	900 mm², 150 mm	**3**	9 m², 12.5 m
4	6000 cm², 340 cm	**5**	625 mm², 100 mm	**6**	45 cm²
7	2800 mm²	**8**	700 cm²	**9**	1.2 m²
10	3150 mm²	**11**	900 mm², 200 mm	**12**	1000 mm²
13	225 mm², 100 mm	**14**	10 m², £57	**15**	45 m², 4.5 litres
16	3200 cm²				

Exercise 4.2 *page 35*

1	55 cm²	**2**	21 cm²	**3**	25 cm²	**4**	780 mm²
5	425 mm²	**6**	1300 mm²	**7**	4.8 m²	**8**	0.6 m²
9	28 cm²	**10**	57 cm²	**11**	100 cm²	**12**	250 mm²
13	650 mm²	**14**	1.8 m²	**15**	0.6 m²	**16**	6000 cm²

17	140 cm²	**18**	800 mm²	**19**	225 mm²	**20**	0.6 m²
21	84 cm²	**22**	300 cm²	**23**	350 mm²	**24**	0.2 m²
25	120 cm²						

Exercise 4.3 *page 37*

1	15 cm²	**2**	28 cm²	**3**	54 cm²	**4**	160 mm²
5	3 m²	**6**	48 cm²	**7**	120 cm²	**8**	300 cm²
9	600 mm²	**10**	2000 mm²	**11**	1000 mm²	**12**	9.6 m²
13	7.5 m²	**14**	5.4 cm²	**15**	27 cm²	**16**	30 m²
17	14 m²	**18**	6 m²	**19**	8 m²	**20**	1.8 cm²

Exercise 4.4 *page 38*

1	6 cm	**2**	8 cm	**3**	7 cm	**4**	3 cm	**5**	9 cm
6	6 cm	**7**	40 mm	**8**	60 mm	**9**	25 mm	**10**	45 mm
11	35 mm	**12**	4 cm	**13**	3 cm	**14**	4 cm	**15**	6 cm
16	3 m	**17**	5 m	**18**	8 m	**19**	2.5 m	**20**	1.5 m

Exercise 4.5 *page 39*

1	12 cm²	**2**	32 cm²	**3**	50 cm²	**4**	60 cm²
5	200 mm²	**6**	2 m²	**7**	26 m²	**8**	8 cm²
9	20 cm²	**10**	84 cm²	**11**	5 m²	**12**	550 mm²

Exercise 4.6 *page 41*

1	40 cm²	**2**	60 cm²	**3**	72 cm²	**4**	60 cm²
5	30 cm²	**6**	300 mm²	**7**	50 mm²	**8**	14 m²
9	56 mm²	**10**	72 cm²	**11**	84 cm²	**12**	840 mm²
13	1200 mm²	**14**	30 cm²	**15**	24 cm²	**16**	72 cm²

Exercise 4.7 *page 43*

1	7 m²	**2**	46 m²	**3**	52 m², 130	**4**	15 m², 12
5	2100 cm²	**6**	160 cm²	**7**	900 cm²	**8**	68 m²
9	168 mm²	**10**	46 cm²	**11**	100 cm², 90 cm², 900 mm², 9 cm²		

Book 4 Unit 5

AT 2/6 (vi)   Pupils formulate and solve linear equations with whole-number coefficients.

AT 2/7 (vii)   Pupils solve simple inequalities.
Implied at Level 6/7: Pupils show an increasing ability to work with algebraic manipulation.
Implied at Level 6/7: Pupils can multiply and divide using negative numbers and substitute these in simple algebraic expressions.

Exercise 5.1 *page 46*

1

$\times$	10	5	0	-5	-10
10	100	50	0	-50	-100
5	50	25	0	-25	-50
0	0	0	0	0	0
-5	-50	-25	0	25	50
-10	-100	-50	0	50	100

2

$\times$	6	3	0	-3	-6
6	36	18	0	-18	-36
3	18	9	0	-9	-18
0	0	0	0	0	0
-3	-18	-9	0	9	18
-6	-36	-18	0	18	36

3

×	4	2	0	−2	−4
8	32	16	0	−16	−32
4	16	8	0	−8	−16
0	0	0	0	0	0
−4	−16	−8	0	8	16
−8	−32	−16	0	16	32

4

×	8	4	0	−4	−8
6	48	24	0	−24	−48
3	24	12	0	−12	−24
0	0	0	0	0	0
−3	−24	−12	0	12	24
−6	−48	−24	0	24	48

5

×	5	2	0	−2	−5
5	25	10	0	−10	−25
2	10	4	0	−4	−10
0	0	0	0	0	0
−2	−10	−4	0	4	10
−5	−25	−10	0	10	25

6

×	−1	−2	−3	−4	−5
−1	1	2	3	4	5
0	0	0	0	0	0
1	−1	−2	−3	−4	−5
2	−2	−4	−6	−8	−10
3	−3	−6	−9	−12	−15

Exercise 5.2 *page 47*

1 60	**2** 8	**3** 18	**4** 30	**5** 32
6 42	**7** 36	**8** 8	**9** 12	**10** 4
11 16	**12** 24	**13** −15	**14** −32	**15** −54
16 −84	**17** −6	**18** −20	**19** −12	**20** −6
21 −8	**22** −24	**23** −35	**24** −72	**25** −33
26 −10	**27** −35	**28** −20	**29** −15	**30** −12
31 $6a$	**32** $20ab$	**33** $30a^2$	**34** $15x$	**35** $28y$
36 $72z$	**37** $8a$	**38** $35b$	**39** $15mn$	**40** $40pq$
41 $28x^2$	**42** $27y^2$	**43** $-21x$	**44** $-45y$	**45** $-44z$
46 $-24a$	**47** $-36b$	**48** $-42uv$	**49** $-60pq$	**50** $-32m^2$
51 $-63n^2$	**52** $-36p$	**53** $-35q$	**54** $-70r$	**55** $-18a$
56 $-108b$	**57** $-56xy$	**58** $-55mn$	**59** $-72t^2$	**60** $-12u^2$

Exercise 5.3 *page 47*

1 5	**2** 4	**3** 4	**4** 3	**5** 4
6 7	**7** 16	**8** 14	**9** 9	**10** 4
11 6	**12** −5	**13** −4	**14** −8	**15** −7
16 −15	**17** −12	**18** −9	**19** −9	**20** −3
21 −3	**22** −5	**23** −9	**24** −9	**25** −14
26 −13	**27** −75	**28** $-4\frac{1}{2}$	**29** $-3\frac{1}{2}$	**30** $-2\frac{1}{2}$
31 5	**32** 4	**33** $6a$	**34** $3a$	**35** $9x$

36 $5y$	**37** $4z$	**38** 7	**39** 5	**40** 9
41 8	**42** 9	**43** 7	**44** $-4x$	**45** $-8y$
46 -6	**47** -6	**48** -4	**49** -6	**50** -5
51 -6	**52** -3	**53** $-8a$	**54** $-3b$	**55** -3
56 -4	**57** -7	**58** $-7s$	**59** $-12c$	**60** $-10d$

Exercise 5.4 *page 48*

1 6	**2** 2	**3** 8	**4** 28	**5** 8	**6** 20
7 8	**8** 8	**9** 16	**10** 4	**11** 16	**12** 32
13 10	**14** 8	**15** 14	**16** 0	**17** 12	**18** 4
19 20	**20** 32	**21** 12	**22** 32	**23** 16	**24** 64
25 8	**26** 2	**27** 20	**28** 15	**29** 11	**30** 17
31 15	**32** 30	**33** 75	**34** 25	**35** 9	**36** 45
37 19	**38** 9	**39** 16	**40** 75	**41** 45	**42** 125
43 27	**44** 54	**45** 59	**46** 100	**47** 225	**48** 450

Exercise 5.5 *page 48*

1 9	**2** 4	**3** 5	**4** -8	**5** -5	**6** -9
7 -8	**8** -10	**9** -8	**10** 10	**11** 2	**12** 1
13 -18	**14** -5	**15** -4	**16** -45	**17** -14	**18** -21
19 14	**20** 9	**21** 8	**22** -15	**23** 5	**24** 11
25 -16	**26** -2	**27** -9	**28** 18	**29** 12	**30** 14
31 -16	**32** 5	**33** 6	**34** -60	**35** -4	**36** -5

Exercise 5.6 *page 49*

1 7	**2** 3	**3** 4	**4** -6	**5** -6	**6** -4
7 -8	**8** -6	**9** -8	**10** -12	**11** -20	**12** -9
13 -9	**14** -7	**15** -5	**16** -9	**17** -9	**18** -8
19 -9	**20** -6	**21** -5	**22** 5	**23** 4	**24** 5
25 6	**26** 20	**27** 5	**28** 4	**29** 8	**30** 12

Exercise 5.7 *page 49*

1 -6	**2** -12	**3** 8	**4** 0	**5** 0	**6** -12
7 32	**8** 0	**9** 0	**10** -36	**11** 24	**12** 0
13 0	**14** 0	**15** 0	**16** 48	**17** 120	**18** 0
19 0	**20** 0	**21** 6	**22** 12	**23** 2	**24** 18
25 3	**26** 6	**27** 12	**28** 54	**29** 24	**30** 10
31 -36	**32** -18	**33** -12	**34** -6	**35** 36	**36** -36
37 -72	**38** -24	**39** 24	**40** 180		

Exercise 5.8 *page 49*

1 4	**2** 80	**3** -8	**4** -16	**5** -32	**6** 64
7 36	**8** 6	**9** -54	**10** -27	**11** -12	**12** 45
13 45	**14** 12	**15** -32	**16** -36	**17** 60	**18** 72
19 32	**20** 54	**21** -81	**22** -48	**23** 72	**24** 144
25 28	**26** 99	**27** -40	**28** 36	**29** -36	**30** 108

Exercise 5.9 *page 50*

1 $9a$	**2** $11b$	**3** $10c$	**4** $3d$
5 $4m$	**6** n	**7** $3p$	**8** $3q$
9 $6r$	**10** s	**11** $5x + 7y$	**12** $9u + 2v$
13 $4a + 5b$	**14** $2c + 3d$	**15** $8m + 4n$	**16** $2z + 7z^2$
17 $5t + 8t^2$	**18** $9a + 7b$	**19** $12c + 7d$	**20** $11m + 8n$
21 $7p + 5q$	**22** $8u + 3v$	**23** $12x + y$	**24** $6a + 5b$
25 $3c + 7d$	**26** $2z^2 + 5z$	**27** $10t^2 + t$	**28** $3a - 2b$
29 $5c - 4d$	**30** $2m - 3n$	**31** $10z^2 - 5z$	**32** $7t^2 - 4t$

33 $3p - 2q$	**34** $4r - s$	**35** $u - v$	**36** $5b - 2a$
37 $4d - 4c$	**38** $4y - 3x$	**39** $5v - 2u$	**40** $3z - 4z^2$
41 $4t - t^2$	**42** $n - m$	**43** $3p - 7q$	**44** $5x - 8y$
45 $5a - 12b$	**46** $11c - 10d$	**47** $2m - 9n$	**48** $p - 10q$
49 $7ab$	**50** $5cd$	**51** $3mn$	**52** rs
53 $2xy$	**54** $5uv$	**55** $5mn$	**56** $7xy$
57 $7pq$	**58** $6uv$	**59** $2ab$	**60** 0

Exercise 5.10   *page 50*

1 $4x + 8$	**2** $5y + 15$	**3** $3z + 12$	**4** $6a + 6b$
5 $2p - 6$	**6** $4q - 8$	**7** $3r - 3$	**8** $5c - 5d$
9 $12 - 3a$	**10** $10 - 5b$	**11** $12 - 4c$	**12** $2v - 2u$
13 $-3m - 6$	**14** $-4n - 20$	**15** $-6p - 6q$	**16** $6x + 4y$
17 $8m + 20n$	**18** $15p + 5q$	**19** $3u + 12v$	**20** $12a - 16b$
21 $15c - 6d$	**22** $12m - 6n$	**23** $5x - 25y$	**24** $9q - 6p$
25 $16s - 20r$	**26** $8v - 24u$	**27** $16b - 2a$	**28** $-30x - 25y$
29 $-9m - 3n$	**30** $-7c - 35d$		

Exercise 5.11   *page 51*

1 $5x + 3y$	**2** $6u + 2v$	**3** $5a + 4b$	**4** $2c + 5d$
5 $4m + 6n$	**6** $4p + 7q$	**7** $2x + 7y$	**8** $6a + 4b$
9 $8c + 2d$	**10** $5m + n$	**11** $5a + 5b$	**12** $6m + 2n$
13 $11p + q$	**14** $10u - 2v$	**15** $13b - 3c$	**16** $11x + 3y$
17 $7a + b$	**18** $7c - 3d$	**19** $10y - 10z$	**20** $2m - 2n$
21 $5p - 5q$	**22** $3x + 3y$	**23** $2c - 12d$	**24** $3m - 9n$
25 $3p - 5q$	**26** $2u + 8v$	**27** $2x + 10y$	**28** $a + 7b$
29 $8m - 8n$	**30** $p - q$		

Exercise 5.12   *page 52*

1 4	**2** 6	**3** 7	**4** 8	**5** 15	**6** 16
7 18	**8** 16	**9** 14	**10** 15	**11** -18	**12** -13
13 -16	**14** -13	**15** -16	**16** -14	**17** -18	**18** -24
19 -25	**20** -20	**21** -17	**22** -16	**23** -19	**24** -29
25 -14	**26** -15	**27** -17	**28** -15	**29** -19	**30** -22
31 15	**32** 18	**33** 24	**34** 21	**35** 17	**36** 25
37 18	**38** 17	**39** 25	**40** 26		

Exercise 5.13   *page 52*

1 2	**2** 6	**3** 4	**4** 1	**5** 8	**6** 4
7 6	**8** 12	**9** 7	**10** 9	**11** 7	**12** 8
13 9	**14** 9	**15** 8	**16** 10	**17** 12	**18** 14
19 18	**20** 20	**21** 4	**22** 3	**23** 4	**24** 5
25 2	**26** 3	**27** 4	**28** 5	**29** 4	**30** 6
31 1	**32** 7	**33** 4	**34** 3	**35** 2	**36** 5
37 7	**38** 2	**39** 6	**40** 4	**41** 7	**42** 3
43 1	**44** 2	**45** 3	**46** 9	**47** 7	**48** 5
49 6	**50** 3	**51** 5	**52** 5	**53** 4	**54** 9
55 4	**56** 5	**57** 6	**58** 6	**59** 3	**60** 5

Exercise 5.14   *page 53*

1 3	**2** 7	**3** 4	**4** 8	**5** 4	**6** 12
7 3	**8** 5	**9** 6	**10** 5	**11** 2	**12** 5
13 5	**14** 7	**15** 3	**16** 5	**17** 1	**18** 5
19 6	**20** 4	**21** 4	**22** 3	**23** 3	**24** 7
25 3	**26** 5	**27** 2	**28** 3	**29** 3	**30** 4

Exercise 5.15   *page 53*

1 $x \leqslant 3$

2 $m > 2$

3 $a < 1$
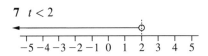

4 $y \geqslant 3$

5 $x \leqslant 4$
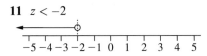

6 $p > 5$

7 $t < 2$
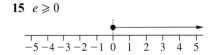

8 $d \geqslant 4$

9 $x \leqslant -3$

10 $f > -3$

11 $z < -2$
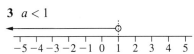

12 $e \leqslant -3$

13 $q > -2$
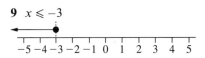

14 $w > 0$
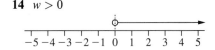

15 $e \geqslant 0$
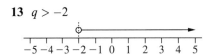

16 $r \geqslant 0$
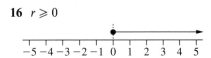

17 $t < 0$
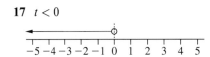

18 $y > -1$
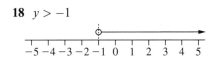

19 $u \leqslant -4$
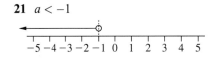

20 $p > -2$
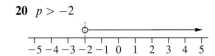

21 $a < -1$
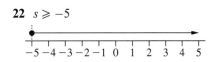

22 $s \geqslant -5$

23 $d \leqslant -3$
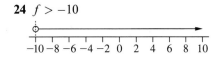

24 $f > -10$

Exercise 5.16   *page 54*

1 $x < -2$

2 $x > 2$

3 $x < 3$

4 $x > 0$
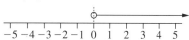

5 $x < 1$

6 $x > -1$
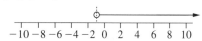

7 $x < -6$

8 $x > 6$

9 $x < -2$

10 $x > -5$

11 $x < 2$

12 $x > 5$

13 $x > -2$
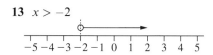

14 $x > 2$

15 $x > -3$
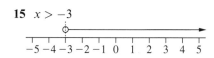

16 $x < 3$
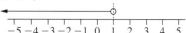

17 $x > -1$
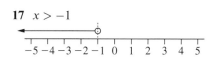

18 $x < 1$

19 $x > -5$
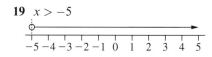

20 $x < 5$

Exercise 5.17   *page 55*   **1** $x > 3$ **2** $y > 4$ **3** $x + y > 5$ **4** $x + y \geqslant 3$ **5** $y \geqslant 2x$

6 $x < 4$ **7** $y < 5$ **8** $y \leqslant 3$ **9** $x + y \leqslant 2$ **10** $y \leqslant \frac{1}{2}x$

Book 4 Unit 6

AT 3/6 (i)	Pupils recognise and use common 2-D representations of 3-D objects.

Exercise 6.4   *page 59*   **1** T, Z   **2** S, X   **3** V, Y   **4** U, W

Book 4 Unit 7

AT 4/6 (v)	When dealing with a combination of two experiments, pupils identify all the outcomes, using diagrammatic, tabular or other forms of communication.
AT 4/6 (vi)	In solving problems, pupils use their knowledge that the total probability of all mutually exclusive outcomes of an experiment is 1.
AT 4/7 (v)	Pupils understand relative frequency as an estimate of probability and use this to compare outcomes of experiments.

Exercise 7.1   *page 65*

1 a $\frac{3}{5} = 0.6$ **b** $\frac{3}{10} = 0.3$ **c** $\frac{1}{10} = 0.1$

2 a $\frac{1}{5} = 0.2$ **b** $\frac{1}{2} = 0.5$ **c** $\frac{3}{10} = 0.3$

3 a $\frac{1}{6} = 0.17$ **b** $\frac{1}{3} = 0.33$ **c** $\frac{1}{12} = 0.08$ **d** $\frac{5}{12} = 0.42$

4 a $\frac{1}{2} = 0.5$ **b** $\frac{2}{5} = 0.4$ **c** $\frac{1}{10} = 0.1$

5 a $\frac{2}{3} = 0.67$ **b** $\frac{1}{4} = 0.25$ **c** $\frac{1}{12} = 0.08$

6 a $\frac{1}{3} = 0.33$ **b** $\frac{1}{4} = 0.25$ **c** $\frac{1}{6} = 0.17$

　 d $\frac{1}{4} = 0.25$ **e** $\frac{7}{12} = 0.58$ **f** $\frac{5}{12} = 0.42$

7 a $\frac{1}{2} = 0.5$ **b** $\frac{2}{3} = 0.67$ **c** $\frac{1}{3} = 0.33$

8 a $\frac{1}{2} = 0.5$ **b** $\frac{1}{2} = 0.5$ **c** 1

9 a $\frac{1}{4} = 0.25$ **b** $\frac{1}{3} = 0.33$ **c** $\frac{1}{6} = 0.17$

　 d $\frac{1}{4} = 0.25$ **e** $\frac{1}{3} = 0.33$

10 a $\frac{1}{4} = 0.25$ **b** $\frac{1}{8} = 0.125$ **c** $\frac{1}{4} = 0.25$ **d** $\frac{3}{8} = 0.375$

　 e $\frac{1}{2} = 0.5$ **f** $\frac{1}{4} = 0.25$ **g** $\frac{1}{4} = 0.25$

Exercise 7.2   *page 67*

1 a

Nicola	two heads	$\frac{6}{20} = 0.3$
	two tails	$\frac{4}{20} = 0.2$
	heads and tails	$\frac{10}{20} = 0.5$
Edward	two heads	$\frac{4}{20} = 0.2$
	two tails	$\frac{9}{20} = 0.45$
	heads and tails	$\frac{7}{20} = 0.35$
Wayne	two heads	$\frac{5}{20} = 0.25$
	two tails	$\frac{4}{20} = 0.2$
	heads and tails	$\frac{11}{20} = 0.55$
Clare	two heads	$\frac{6}{20} = 0.3$
	two tails	$\frac{2}{20} = 0.1$
	heads and tails	$\frac{12}{20} = 0.6$

Madrina   two heads $\frac{2}{20} = 0.1$

two tails $\frac{5}{20} = 0.25$

heads and tails $\frac{13}{20} = 0.65$

b Combined   two heads $\frac{23}{100} = 0.23$

results   two tails $\frac{24}{100} = 0.24$

heads and tails $\frac{53}{100} = 0.53$

c The combined results.

2 a Student A   3 $\frac{3}{25} = 0.12$ Student B   3 $\frac{4}{25} = 0.16$

     4   $\frac{5}{25} = 0.2$ 4 $\frac{5}{25} = 0.2$

     5   $\frac{11}{25} = 0.44$ 5 $\frac{6}{25} = 0.24$

     6   $\frac{3}{25} = 0.12$ 6 $\frac{7}{25} = 0.28$

     7   $\frac{2}{25} = 0.08$ 7 $\frac{3}{25} = 0.12$

     8   $\frac{1}{25} = 0.04$ 8   0

Student C   3 $\frac{1}{25} = 0.04$ Student D   3 $\frac{2}{25} = 0.08$

     4   $\frac{8}{25} = 0.32$ 4 $\frac{4}{25} = 0.16$

     5   $\frac{5}{25} = 0.2$ 5 $\frac{7}{25} = 0.28$

     6   $\frac{6}{25} = 0.24$ 6 $\frac{8}{25} = 0.32$

     7   0   7 $\frac{4}{25} = 0.16$

     8   $\frac{5}{25} = 0.2$ 8   0

b Combined results   3 $\frac{10}{100} = 0.1$

     4   $\frac{22}{100} = 0.22$

     5   $\frac{29}{100} = 0.29$

     6   $\frac{24}{100} = 0.24$

     7   $\frac{9}{100} = 0.09$

     8   $\frac{6}{100} = 0.06$

c The combined results.   **d** 290   **e** 640

3 a Officer A   38 $\frac{2}{20} = 0.1$ Officer B   38 $\frac{1}{20} = 0.05$

     39   $\frac{6}{20} = 0.3$ 39 $\frac{5}{20} = 0.25$

     40   $\frac{7}{20} = 0.35$ 40 $\frac{8}{20} = 0.4$

     41   $\frac{5}{20} = 0.25$ 41 $\frac{5}{20} = 0.25$

     42   0   42 $\frac{1}{20} = 0.05$

Officer C   38   0   Officer D   38 $\frac{3}{20} = 0.15$

     39   $\frac{4}{20} = 0.2$ 39 $\frac{4}{20} = 0.2$

     40   $\frac{12}{20} = 0.6$ 40 $\frac{5}{20} = 0.25$

     41   $\frac{4}{20} = 0.2$ 41 $\frac{7}{20} = 0.35$

     42   0   42 $\frac{1}{20} = 0.05$

Officer E   38 $\frac{1}{20} = 0.05$

39    $\frac{8}{20} = 0.4$

40    $\frac{10}{20} = 0.5$

41   0

42    $\frac{1}{20} = 0.05$

b Combined results   38 $\frac{7}{100} = 0.07$

39    $\frac{27}{100} = 0.27$

40    $\frac{42}{100} = 0.42$

41    $\frac{21}{100} = 0.21$

42    $\frac{3}{100} = 0.03$

c The combined results.   **d** 420   **e** 480

4 a Group A   R $\frac{21}{50} = 0.42$ Group B   R $\frac{17}{50} = 0.34$

B $\frac{12}{50} = 0.24$ B $\frac{18}{50} = 0.36$

G $\frac{7}{50} = 0.14$ G $\frac{5}{50} = 0.1$

Y $\frac{10}{50} = 0.2$ Y $\frac{10}{50} = 0.2$

Group C   R $\frac{28}{50} = 0.56$ Group D   R $\frac{20}{50} = 0.4$

B $\frac{13}{50} = 0.26$ B $\frac{16}{50} = 0.32$

G $\frac{7}{50} = 0.14$ G $\frac{11}{50} = 0.22$

Y $\frac{2}{50} = 0.04$ Y $\frac{3}{50} = 0.06$

b Combined results   R $\frac{86}{200} = 0.43$

B $\frac{59}{200} = 0.295$

G $\frac{30}{200} = 0.15$

Y $\frac{25}{200} = 0.125$

c The combined results.   **d** 645   **e** 2850

Exercise 7.3   *page 69*   **1 a** 500   **b** 500   **c** 1000

2 a

second spinner			
5	6	7	8
4	5	6	7
3	4	5	6
2	3	4	5
1	2	3	4
	1	2	3

first spinner

b $\frac{6}{15} = 0.4$ **c** $\frac{3}{15} = 0.2$

3 a

second spinner			
6	7	9	11
4	5	7	9
2	3	5	7
	1	3	5

first spinner

b $\frac{6}{9} = 0.67$ **c** $\frac{2}{9} = 0.22$

4 a

second spinner			
4	4	8	12
3	3	6	9
2	2	4	6
1	1	2	3
	1	2	3

first spinner

b $\frac{5}{12} = 0.42$ **c** $\frac{8}{12} = 0.67$ **d** (i) 200   (ii) 100

5 a

second spinner			
5	5	10	15
4	4	8	12
3	3	6	9
2	2	4	6
1	1	2	3
	1	2	3

first spinner

b (i) $\frac{1}{5} = 0.07$ (ii) $\frac{2}{15} = 0.13$ (iii) $\frac{2}{15} = 0.13$ (iv) $\frac{2}{15} = 0.13$

(v) $\frac{1}{15} = 0.07$ (vi) $\frac{2}{15} = 0.13$ (vii) $\frac{1}{15} = 0.07$ (viii) $\frac{1}{15} = 0.07$

(ix) $\frac{1}{15} = 0.07$ (x) $\frac{1}{15} = 0.07$

c (i) 133   (ii) 67

6 a

second die						
6	7	8	9	10	11	12
5	6	7	8	9	10	11
4	5	6	7	8	9	10
3	4	5	6	7	8	9
2	3	4	5	6	7	8
1	2	3	4	5	6	7
	1	2	3	4	5	6

first die

b (i) 0   (ii) $\frac{1}{36} = 0.03$ (iii) $\frac{2}{36} = 0.06$ (iv) $\frac{3}{36} = 0.08$

(v) $\frac{4}{36} = 0.11$ (vi) $\frac{5}{36} = 0.14$ (vii) $\frac{6}{36} = 0.16$ (viii) $\frac{5}{36} = 0.14$

(ix) $\frac{4}{36} = 0.11$ (x) $\frac{3}{36} = 0.08$ (xi) $\frac{2}{36} = 0.06$ (xii) $\frac{1}{36} = 0.03$

(xiii) $\frac{18}{36} = 0.5$ (xiv) $\frac{12}{36} = 0.33$ (xv) $\frac{26}{36} = 0.72$

c (i) 100   (ii) 600

7 a

second cut				
C	HC	DC	SC	CC
S	HS	DS	SS	CS
D	HD	DD	SD	CD
H	HH	DH	SH	CH
	H	D	S	C

first cut

b (i) $\frac{1}{16} = 0.0625$ (ii) $\frac{2}{16} = 0.125$ (iii) $\frac{8}{16} = 0.5$

(iv) $\frac{6}{16} = 0.375$ (v) $\frac{7}{16} = 0.4375$

c 900

8 a

3	M	M	M	M	M	M
2	M	M	M	M	D	D
1	M	M	D	D	W	W
0	D	D	W	W	W	W
0	D	D	W	W	W	W
0	D	D	W	W	W	W
	0	0	1	1	2	2

Mary (left)   William (bottom)

b $\frac{14}{36} \times 360 = 140$

Exercise 7.4   *page 71*

1 a $\frac{1}{3} = 0.33$ b $\frac{2}{3} = 0.67$ c $\frac{1}{9} = 0.11$ d $\frac{1}{9} = 0.11$ e $\frac{1}{9} = 0.11$

2 a $\frac{1}{3} = 0.33$ b $\frac{2}{3} = 0.67$ c $\frac{4}{9} = 0.44$

3 a $\frac{1}{3} = 0.33$ b $\frac{4}{9} = 0.44$ c $\frac{4}{9} = 0.44$ d $\frac{1}{9} = 0.44$

4 a $\frac{1}{3} = 0.33$ b $\frac{4}{9} = 0.44$ c $\frac{1}{9} = 0.11$

5 a $\frac{1}{9} = 0.11$ b $\frac{4}{9} = 0.44$ c $\frac{4}{9} = 0.44$ d $\frac{4}{9} = 0.44$

6 a $\frac{4}{9} = 0.44$ b $\frac{1}{9} = 0.11$ c $\frac{4}{9} = 0.44$

7 a $\frac{5}{9} = 0.56$ b $\frac{4}{9} = 0.44$ c $\frac{1}{9} = 0.11$

8 a $\frac{5}{9} = 0.56$ b $\frac{4}{9} = 0.44$ c 1

9 a $\frac{4}{9} = 0.44$ b $\frac{4}{9} = 0.44$

10 a $\frac{1}{4} = 0.25$ b $\frac{1}{4} = 0.25$ c $\frac{1}{4} = 0.25$ d $\frac{9}{16} = 0.5625$ e 1

Exercise 7.5   *page 73*

1 a $\frac{1}{3} = 0.33$ b $\frac{2}{3} = 0.67$ c $\frac{2}{3} = 0.67$

2 a $\frac{1}{3} = 0.33$ b $\frac{2}{3} = 0.67$ c $\frac{2}{3} = 0.67$

3 a $\frac{1}{3} = 0.33$ b $\frac{2}{3} = 0.67$ c 1

4 a $\frac{1}{3} = 0.33$ b $\frac{1}{3} = 0.33$

5 a $\frac{1}{3} = 0.33$ b $\frac{2}{3} = 0.67$

6 a $\frac{1}{3} = 0.33$ b $\frac{1}{3} = 0.33$

7 a $\frac{1}{3} = 0.33$ b $\frac{2}{3} = 0.67$

8 a $\frac{1}{2} = 0.5$ b $\frac{1}{3} = 0.33$

9 a $\frac{1}{2} = 0.5$ b $\frac{1}{6} = 0.17$ c $\frac{1}{6} = 0.17$ d $\frac{1}{2} = 0.5$

10 a $\frac{1}{2} = 0.5$ b $\frac{1}{6} = 0.17$ c $\frac{1}{6} = 0.17$

Book 4   Unit 8

AT 2/6 (vii)   Pupils represent mappings expressed algebraically, interpreting general features and using graphical representation in four quadrants where appropriate.

Implied at Level 6 Pupils use and interpret co-ordinates in all four quadrants.

Exercise 8.1   *page 76*

A (1, 2),   B (1, 5),   C (1, −2),   D (1, −3),   E (2, 0),   F (2, 4),
G (2, −1),   H (2, −3),   I (4, 0),   J (4, 3),   K (4, −2),   L (4, −5),
M (−1, 0),   N (−1, 2),   P (−1, 3),   Q (−1, −2),   R (−1, −5),   S (−3, 1),
T (−3, 4),   U (−3, −1),   V (−3, −3),   W (−5, 0),   X (−5, 5),   Y (−5, −4),
Z (0, −4)

Exercise 8.2 *page 77*

1 cricket bat   **2** christmas tree   **3** rolling pin   **4** arrow
5 compass and pencil   **6** cup and saucer   **7** tank
8 elephant   **9** horse   **10** windmill   **11** flag

Exercise 8.3 *page 78*

1

	A	B	C	D	E	F
x	−2	−1	0	1	2	3
y	−7	−5	−3	−1	1	3

2

	A	B	C	D	E	F
x	−3	−2	−1	0	1	2
y	−2	0	2	4	6	8

3

	A	B	C	D	E	F
x	−2	−1	0	1	2	3
y	−8	−6	−4	−2	0	2

4

	A	B	C	D	E	F	G
x	−3	−2	−1	0	1	2	3
y	−8	−5	−2	1	4	7	10

Exercise 8.5 *page 80*

1 $y = 1, 3, 5, 7$ and 9 **2** $y = 4, 6, 8, 10$ and 12
3 $y = -5, -1, 3, 7$ and 11 **4** $y = -7, -3, 1, 5$ and 9
5 $y = -9, -5, -1, 3$ and 7 **6** $y = -11, -7, -3, 1$ and 5
7 $y = -8, -3, 2, 7$ and 12

Exercise 8.6 *page 81*

1

x	−2	−1	0	1	2
$2x$	−4	−2	0	2	4
−2	−2	−2	−2	−2	−2
y	−6	−4	−2	0	2

2

x	−2	−1	0	1	2
$3x$	−6	−3	0	3	6
−1	−1	−1	−1	−1	−1
y	−7	−4	−1	2	5

3

x	−2	−1	0	1	2
x	−2	−1	0	1	2
−1	−1	−1	−1	−1	−1
y	−3	−2	−1	0	1

4

x	−2	−1	0	1	2
x	−2	−1	0	1	2
+2	+2	+2	+2	+2	+2
y	0	1	2	3	4

5

x	−2	−1	0	1	2
$2x$	−4	−2	0	2	4
+3	+3	+3	+3	+3	+3
y	−1	+1	3	5	7

6

x	−2	−1	0	1	2
$3x$	−6	−3	0	3	6
+2	+2	+2	+2	+2	+2
y	−4	−1	2	5	8

7

x	−2	−1	0	1	2
$3x$	−6	−3	0	3	6
+4	+4	+4	+4	+4	+4
y	−2	1	4	7	10

8

x	−2	−1	0	1	2
$2x$	−4	−2	0	2	4
+2	+2	+2	+2	+2	+2
y	−2	0	2	4	6

9

x	−2	−1	0	1	2
$y = 2x$	−4	−2	0	2	4

10

x	−2	−1	0	1	2
$2x$	−4	−2	0	2	4
−1	−1	−1	−1	−1	−1
y	−5	−3	−1	1	3

11

x	−2	−1	0	1	2
$3x$	−6	−3	0	3	6
−3	−3	−3	−3	−3	−3
y	−9	−6	−3	0	3

12

x	−2	−1	0	1	2
$3x$	−6	−3	0	3	6
−1	−1	−1	−1	−1	−1
y	−7	−4	−1	2	5

13	x	-2	-1	0	1	2
	$y = 4x$	-8	-4	0	4	8

14	x	-2	-1	0	1	2
	$4x$	-8	-4	0	4	8
	-2	-2	-2	-2	-2	-2
	y	-10	-6	-2	2	6

15	x	-2	-1	0	1	2
	$y = 5x$	-10	-5	0	5	10

Book 4   Unit 9

AT 4/6 (iv)	Pupils draw conclusions from scatter diagrams, and have a basic understanding of correlation.
AT 4/7 (iv)	Pupils draw a line of best fit on a scatter diagram, by inspection.

Exercise 9.1   *page 83*

1	**b**	positive correlation	2	**b**	positive correlation
3	**b**	no correlation	4	**b**	negative correlation
5	**b**	no correlation	6	**b**	positive correlation

Exercise 9.2   *page 87*

1 **a** negative correlation
  b (i) 27 mpg   (ii) 17 mpg   (iii) 12 mpg   (iv) 35 mpg
  c (i) 1750 cc   (ii) 4750 cc   (iii) 2500 cc

2 **a** positive correlation
  b (i) 120 mph (ii) 140 mph (iii) 160 mph (iv) 100 mph
  c (i) 1000 cc   (ii) 2750 cc   (iii) 500 cc   (iv) 1600 cc

3 **b** positive correlation
  d (i) 2.5 A   (ii) 5.5 A   (iii) 7.5 A   (iv) 1.5 A
  e (i) 5 V   (ii) 35 V   (iii) 65 V   (iv) 87 V

4 **b** negative correlation
  d (i) 30 hours (ii) 26 hours (iii) 21 hours (iv) 16 hours
  e (i) 34 hours (ii) 26 hours

5 **b** positive correlation
  d (i) 3.4 cm   (ii) 5.1 cm   (iii) 7.5 cm   (iv) 2.5 cm
  e (i) 1000 litres (ii) 4900 litres (iii) 2800 litres (iv) 4400 litres

6 **b** positive correlation
  d (i) 1.2 s   (ii) 1.4 s   (iii) 1.6 s   (iv) 1.8 s
     (to 1 dp)
  e (i) 25 cm   (ii) 65 cm

Book 5 Unit 1

AT 3/7 (i)   Pupils understand and apply Pythagoras' theorem when solving problems in two dimensions.

Exercise 1.1 *page 1*

1 400	**2** 169	**3** 196	**4** 324	**5** 484	**6** 676
7 729	**8** 841	**9** 961	**10** 1600	**11** 3600	**12** 4900
13 1225	**14** 4225	**15** 5625	**16** 10 000	**17** 1156	**18** 1681
19 2304	**20** 3136	**21** 3969	**22** 6084	**23** 8281	**24** 9604

Exercise 1.2 *page 1*

1 30	**2** 15	**3** 25	**4** 16	**5** 17	**6** 19	**7** 21	**8** 23
9 24	**10** 28	**11** 50	**12** 80	**13** 90	**14** 45	**15** 55	**16** 85
17 32	**18** 44	**19** 54	**20** 61	**21** 72	**22** 84	**23** 81	**24** 99

Exercise 1.3 *page 2*

1 25	**2** 26	**3** 34	**4** 50	**5** 29	**6** 53	**7** 41	**8** 61
9 37	**10** 100	**11** 8	**12** 12	**13** 15	**14** 60	**15** 24	**16** 40
17 60	**18** 80	**19** 70	**20** 29				

Exercise 1.4 *page 2*

1 72 m   **2** 104 cm   **3** 132 cm   **4** 300 cm   **5** no, the error is +4 m

Exercise 1.5 *page 3*

1 3721 cm²   **2** 75 m, 5625 m²   **3** 24 m, 6 m, 36 m²
4 100 cm, 96 cm, 24 cm, 3 cm, 9 cm², 576 cm²
5 40 cm, 1600 cm²   **6** 2025 cm²   **7** 5400 cm²

Exercise 1.6 *page 4*

1 12 mm, 16 mm, 20 mm   **2** 16 mm, 30 mm, 34 mm
3 20 mm, 21 mm, 29 mm   **4** 9 mm, 40 mm, 41 mm
5 11 mm, 60 mm, 61 mm   **6** 12 mm, 35 mm, 37 mm

Exercise 1.7 *page 4*

1 81, 1600, 1681, 1681   **2** 121, 3600, 3721, 3721
3 144, 1225, 1369, 1369   **4** 144, 256, 400, 400
5 400, 441, 841, 841   **6** 25, 144, 169, 169
7 256, 900, 1156, 1156   **8** 900, 1600, 2500, 2500
9 169, 7056, 7225, 7225   **10** 784, 9216, 10 000, 10 000

Exercise 1.8 *page 5*

1 15 cm	**2** 17 cm	**3** 26 cm	**4** 40 cm	**5** 50 mm
6 100 cm	**7** 90 cm	**8** 75 mm	**9** 65 mm	**10** 45 mm
11 75 cm	**12** 65 cm	**13** 85 cm	**14** 1 m	

Exercise 1.9 *page 6*

1 2.56 m   **2** 1.70 m   **3** 47.17 km   **4** 781.02 m   **5** 4.52 m
6 1.52 m   **7** yes (diagonal = 1.12 m)   **8** 123.81 m

Exercise 1.10 *page 7*

1 7 cm	**2** 20 cm	**3** 40 cm	**4** 80 mm	**5** 16 mm
6 45 mm	**7** 36 cm	**8** 35 cm	**9** $1\frac{1}{5}$ m	**10** $\frac{2}{5}$ m
11 20 cm	**12** 15 cm	**13** 18 cm	**14** 40 mm	**15** 30 mm
16 70 mm	**17** 21 cm	**18** 45 cm	**19** 48 cm	**20** $1\frac{1}{5}$ m

Exercise 1.11 *page 8*

1 $2\frac{1}{2}$ m	**2** 96 m	**3** 30 mm	**4** 25 mm
5 10 cm	**6** 12.60 km	**7** 2.4 m	**8** 52.92 m

Book 5 Unit 2

At 3/6 (vii)	Pupils enlarge shapes by a positive whole-number scale factor.
AT 3/7 (iii)	Pupils enlarge shapes by a fractional scale factor.
AT 3/8 (i)	Pupils understand and use mathematical similarity.

From the Programe of Study:

3d Pupils should be taught to develop an understanding of scale, including using and interpreting maps and drawings, and enshapes by different scale factors; develop an understanding of and use mathematical similarity.

Exercise 2.1 *page 9*

1 c	**2** b	**3** a	**4** b	**5** c	**6** a
7 c	**8** b	**9** c	**10** a	**11** c	**12** b

Exercise 2.2 *page 13*

1 a and b	**2** b and c	**3** b and c	**4** a and c	**5** a and c
6 b and c	**7** a and b	**8** b and c	**9** a and b	**10** a and c
11 a and b	**12** b and c	**13** b and c	**14** a and c	**15** b and c

Exercise 2.3 *page 17*

1 QR = 10 cm, XZ = 11 cm
2 EF = 6 cm, AD = 4 cm, HG = 15 cm
3 JF = 8 cm, AE = 3 cm, BC = 3 cm, CD = 4 cm
4 ST = 9 cm, TU = 6 cm, UV = 4.5 cm, MN = 5 cm, RM = 7 cm
5 PI = 2.5 cm, IJ = 5 cm, JK = 7.5 cm, NO = 15 cm, CD = 4 cm,
DE = 5 cm, EF = 1 cm
6 a $x = 1.5$ m, $y = 2.4$ m, $z = 2.5$ m
b A area = 1.2 m^2 B area = 2.7 m^2 C area = 4.8 m^2 D area = 7.5 m^2
c 1:4
7 a $x = 6$ m, $y = 4$ m, $z = 10$ m
b A area = 4 m^2 B area = 9 m^2 C area = 16 m^2 D area = 25 m^2
c 4:25
8 a 2.8 cm   **b** 2 m by 3 m   **c** 1:10 000   **d** 8 m^2

Exercise 2.6 *page 25*

1 1:100	**2** 1:500	**3** 1:200	**4** 1:2000	**5** 1:5000
6 1:2500	**7** 1:10 000	**8** 1:50	**9** 1:20	**10** 1:25
11 1:100 000	**12** 1:500 000	**13** 1:200 000	**14** 1:20 000	**15** 1:25 000

Exercise 2.7 *page 25*

1 120 cm by 90 cm	**2** 80 cm by 200 cm	**3** 250 cm by 125 cm
4 18 m	**5** 15 m by 12 m	**6** 10 m, 4 m and 2 m
7 12 m, 9 m and 7.5 m	**8** 60 m **9** 70 m	**10** 1:2000, 120 m

Exercise 2.8 *page 26*

1 20 cm by 10 cm	**2** 20 cm by 12 cm	**3** 36 cm
4 6 cm	**5** 20 cm by 12 cm	**6** 8 cm by 5 cm
7 20 cm by 15 cm by 10 cm	**8** 24 cm	**9** 8 cm
10 1:1200, 7 cm		

Exercise 2.9 *page 27*	**1** 040°	**2** 070°	**3** 130°	**4** 150°	**5** 180°			
	6 210°	**7** 260°	**8** 240°	**9** 200°	**10** 220°			
	11 330°	**12** 290°	**13** 320°	**14** 280°	**15** 340°			

Exercise 2.10   *page 28*

1 b 100 km, 270° **2 b** 70 km, 270° **3 b** 80 km, 270° **4 b** 80 km, 270°
5 b 40 km, 270° **6 b** 140 km, 90° **7 b** 50 km, 90° **8 b** 100 km, 90°
9 b 120 km, 90° **10 b** 140 km, 90°

Book 5   Unit 3

AT 4/6 (i)	Pupils collect and record continuous data, choosing appropriate equal class intervals over a sensible range to create frequency tables.
AT 4/6 (ii)	Pupils construct and interpret frequency diagrams.
AT 4/8 (i)	Pupils construct and interpret cumulative frequency tables and diagrams, using the upper boundary of the class interval.
AT 4/7 (ii)	Pupils determine the modal class and estimate the mean, median and range of sets of grouped data, selecting the statistic most appropriate to their line of enquiry.
AT 4/7 (iii)	Pupils use measures of average and range, with associated frequency polygons, as appropriate, to compare distributions and make inferences.
AT 4/8 (ii)	Pupils estimate the median and interquartile range and use these to compare distributions and make inferences.

Exercise 3.1   *page 32*

1 a 17   **b** 42   **c** 100

d

time (minutes)	frequency
15–17	10
17–19	17
19–21	31
21–23	27
23–25	15

e 17–19   **f** 27

2 a

break	frequency
11–20	8
21–30	11
31–40	15
41–50	20
51–60	17
61–70	12
71–80	8
81–90	5
91–100	3
101–110	0
111–120	1
121–130	0
131–140	0

b 17   **c** 17   **d** 54   **e** no   **f** 111–120

3 a 5   **b** 5   **c** 10   **d** 153.5–154.5   **e** 30

f

height (cm)	frequency
148.5–149.5	0
149.5–150.5	1
150.5–151.5	1
151.5–152.5	3
152.5–153.5	4
153.5–154.5	5
154.5–155.5	6
155.5–156.5	4
156.5–157.5	3
157.5–158.5	2
158.5–159.5	1
159.5–160.5	0

4 a

weight (kg)	frequency
23.5–24.5	10
24.5–25.5	15
25.5–26.5	20
26.5–27.5	25
27.5–28.5	15
28.5–29.5	5

b 90   **c** 45   **d** 45   **e** no   **f** 26.5–27.5 kg

5

mark	frequency
1–2	7
3–4	9
5–6	10
7–8	11
9–10	7
11–12	9
13–14	15
15–16	16
17–18	9
19–20	7

6

mark	frequency
1–4	16
5–8	21
9–12	16
13–16	31
17–20	16

10

height (to the nearest cm)	frequency Set 1	Set 2
1	0	0
2	4	0
3	21	3
4	19	9
5	5	9
6	0	17
7	1	10
8	0	2

11

mark	frequency	
	group 1	group 2
1–10	0	0
11–20	5	1
21–30	5	4
31–40	23	7
41–50	9	4
51–60	12	13
61–70	11	12
71–80	5	22
81–90	8	13
91–100	2	4

Exercise 3.2   *page 40*

1

score	1–2	3–4	5–6	7–8	9–10
frequency	7	9	10	11	7

score	11–12	13–14	15–16	17–18	19–20
frequency	9	15	16	9	7

   a modal class 15–16
      range 19
   b median 11.5

2

score	1–4	5–8	9–12	13–16	17–20
frequency	16	21	16	31	16

   a modal class 13–16
      range 19
   b median 11.5

3 a Bill: modal class   61–80
                  range   179
       Terri: modal class   41–60
                  range   159
   b Bill: median   71
       Terri: median   58
   c Bill is better player, higher average score, more evenly spread across whole range.

4 a Before: modal class   100 kg–105 kg
                  range   40 kg
       After: modal class   100 kg–105 kg
                  range   40 kg
   b Before: median   104.5 kg
       After: median   98.5 kg
   c Modal class and range are the same before and after. The median average is 6 kg lighter after the tournament.

5 a Group 1:   modal class   £201–£205
                   range   £399
       Group 2:   modal class   £251–£300
                   range   £299

    b Group 1:   median   £205
        Group 2:   median   £255
    c Group 2 earn more 'on average' and have a smaller range than group 1.

Exercise 3.3 *page 41*

1 a Gilbey's Corner: median   10.5 cm
       Teacher's Nook: median   22.0 cm
  b Gilbey's Corner: lower quartile   7.0 cm
                           upper quartile   14.5 cm
       Teacher's Nook: lower quartile   19.0 cm
                           upper quartile   24.0 cm
  c Gilbey's Corner: inter-quartile range 7.5 cm
       Teacher's Nook: inter-quartile range 5.0 cm

2 a Year 7:   median   240 p
       Year 8:   median   350 p
  b Year 7:   lower quartile   140 p
                   upper quartile   340 p
       Year 8:   lower quartile   260 p
                   upper quartile   440 p
  c Year 7:   inter-quartile range 200 p
       Year 8:   inter-quartile range 180 p

3 a Group 1:   median   53
       Group 2:   median   41
  b Group 1:   lower quartile   38
                   upper quartile   66
       Group 2:   lower quartile   28
                   upper quartile   53
  c Group 1:   inter-quartile range 28
       Group 2:   inter-quartile range 25

4 a Sample 1:   median   480 hours
       Sample 2:   median   420 hours
  b Sample 1:   lower quartile   390 hours
                   upper quartile   580 hours
       Sample 2:   lower quartile   330 hours
                   upper quartile   510 hours
  c Sample 1:   inter-quartile range 190 hours
       Sample 2:   inter-quartile range 180 hours

Exercise 3.4 *page 43*

1 Estimated mean = 10.94
2 Estimated mean = 10.9
3 Estimated mean   Bill: 74.9
                     Terri: 65.3
4 Estimated mean   Before: 102.83 kg
                     After: 96.58 kg
5 Estimated mean   Group 1: £198.50
                     Group 2: £253.50

Exercise 3.5 *page 44*

1 b Worker 1:   modal class   11 miles–15 miles
                 range   34 miles
       Worker 2:   modal class   1 mile–5 miles
                 range   29 miles

    c Worker 1:   median   13 miles
                         lower quartile   9 miles
                         upper quartile   18 miles
        Worker 2:   median   8 miles
                         lower quartile   3 miles
                         upper quartile   14 miles
    d Estimated mean   Worker 1:   14.7 miles
                              Worker 2:   9.85 miles

2 b Group 1:   modal class   51–60
                range   99
      Group 2:   modal class   41–50
                range   89
    c Group 1:   median   55
                lower quartile   41
                upper quartile   69
      Group 2:   median   43
                lower quartile   30
                upper quartile   56
    d Estimated mean   Group 1:   55.1
                              Group 2:   42.5

3 b Sample 1:   modal class   3.5 cm–4.5 cm
                range   7 cm
      Sample 2:   modal class   4.5 cm–5.5 cm
                range   4 cm
    c Sample 1:   median   4.0 cm
                lower quartile   3.2 cm
                upper quartile   5.0 cm
      Sample 2:   median   4.5 cm
                lower quartile   3.5 cm
                upper quartile   5.3 cm
    d Estimated mean   Sample 1:   4.21 cm
                              Sample 2:   4.35 cm

Book 5 Unit 4

AT 3/6 (iv)	Pupils understand and use appropriate formulae for finding the areas of plane rectilinear figures.
AT 3/6 (v)	Pupils understand and use appropriate formulae for finding the circumferences and areas of circles.
AT 3/6 (vi)	Pupils understand and use appropriate formulae for finding the volumes of cuboids.
AT 3/7 (ii)	Pupils calculate lengths, areas and volumes in plane shapes and right prisms.
AT 3/8 (iii)	Pupils distinguish between formulae for perimeter, area and volume by considering dimensions.

Exercise 4.2 *page 45*

1 66 cm	**2** 110 cm	**3** 154 cm	**4** 198 cm
5 242 mm	**6** 440 mm	**7** 220 cm	**8** 88 cm
9 132 cm	**10** 176 cm	**11** 264 mm	**12** 660 mm
13 28.26 cm	**14** 62.8 mm	**15** 37.68 mm	**16** 25.12 cm
17 21.98 cm	**18** 15.7 cm		

Exercise 4.3 *page 46*			
1 $12.56 \, cm^2$	2 $50.24 \, cm^2$	3 $28.26 \, cm^2$	4 $78.5 \, cm^2$
5 $0.0314 \, m^2$	6 $0.125 \, 68 \, m^2$	7 $0.7855 \, m^2$	8 $0.282 \, 78 \, m^2$
9 $0.502 \, 72 \, m^2$	10 $314.2 \, mm^2$	11 $2790 \, mm^2$	12 $1240 \, mm^2$
13 $25 \, 110 \, mm^2$	14 $11 \, 160 \, mm^2$	15 $15 \, 400 \, mm^2$	16 $38.5 \, cm^2$
17 $616 \, cm^2$	18 $1386 \, cm^2$	19 $1.54 \, m^2$	20 $6.16 \, m^2$

Exercise 4.4 *page 46*			
1 2200 cm, 22 m	2 785 m	3 15	
4 5	5 $78.5 \, mm^2$	6 $2464 \, cm^2$	

Exercise 4.5 *page 47*					
1 400 m	2 200 m	3 500 cm	4 400 cm	5 25 m	6 200 m
7 130 cm, 320 mm		8 150 cm, 110 cm, 56 cm		9 260 mm	

Exercise 4.6 *page 49*		
1 8	2 $66 \, mm^2$	3 $314 \, cm^2$, $2512 \, cm^2$, $5024 \, cm^2$, $7536 \, cm^2$
4 Both $616 \, cm^2$	5 $3850 \, mm^2$	6 $3250 \, cm^2$
7 $86 \, mm^2$, $118 \, cm^2$	8 $30 \, cm^2$, $90 \, cm^2$	9 $98 \, cm^2$, $91 \, cm^2$
10 $297 \, cm^2$		

Exercise 4.7 *page 51*			
1 hexagonal	2 octagonal	3 pentagonal	4 square
5 cube	6 rhomboid	7 trapezoid	8 square

Exercise 4.8 *page 52*			
1 $72 \, cm^3$	2 $270 \, cm^3$	3 $90 \, cm^3$	4 $80 \, cm^3$
5 $1000 \, mm^3$	6 $480 \, mm^3$	7 $12 \, m^3$	8 $50 \, cm^3$
9 $240 \, cm^3$	10 $105 \, cm^3$	11 $96 \, cm^3$	12 $144 \, cm^3$
13 $360 \, mm^3$	14 $240 \, mm^3$	15 $3080 \, cm^3$	16 $462 \, cm^3$
17 $628 \, cm^3$	18 $251 \, cm^3$	19 $198 \, cm^3$	20 $11 \, 000 \, mm^3$

Exercise 4.9 *page 54*			
1 $55 \, cm^3$	2 $180 \, cm^3$	3 $128 \, cm^3$	4 $95 \, cm^3$
5 $44 \, cm^3$	6 $96 \, cm^3$	7 $144 \, cm^3$	8 $480 \, cm^3$

Exercise 4.10 *page 55*					
1 30	2 24	3 36	4 24	5 80	6 125

Exercise 4.11 *page 56*			
1 $12 \, 000 \, l$	2 $25 \, 000 \, l$	3 $12 \, l$	4 $36 \, l$
5 $60 \, l$	6 $11 \, l$	7 $198 \, 000 \, l$	8 $314 \, 000 \, l$
9 **a** $840 \, l$ **b** 10 weeks		10 **a** $27 \, l$ **b** 135	
11 **a** $308 \, l$ **b** 11		12 **a** $44 \, l$ **b** 200	
13 $24 \, cm^3$	14 $300 \, 000 \, cm^3$	15 $24 \, m^2$	16 $1440 \, m^3$
17 $98 \, m^3$			

Exercise 4.12 *page 58*			
1 volume	2 perimeter	3 area	4 perimeter
5 area	6 volume	7 area	8 volume
9 perimeter	10 area	11 volume	12 perimeter
13 volume	14 area	15 volume	16 area
17 perimeter	18 area	19 area	20 perimeter

Book 5   Unit 6

AT 2/7 (ii)	Pupils understand the effects of multiplying and dividing by numbers between 0 and 1.
AT 2/7 (iv)	Pupils understand and use proportional change.
AT 2/8 (ii)	Pupils choose to use fractions or percentages to solve problems involving repeated proportional changes or the calculation of the original quantity given the result of a proportional change.

Exercise 6.1 *page 64*   1 $\frac{31}{100}$ 2 $\frac{7}{10}$ 3 $\frac{1}{10}$ 4 $\frac{2}{5}$ 5 $\frac{3}{5}$ 6 $\frac{1}{2}$
    7 $\frac{3}{4}$ 8 $\frac{9}{20}$ 9 $\frac{11}{20}$ 10 $\frac{1}{20}$ 11 29%   12 81%
    13 7%   14 30%   15 90%   16 15%   17 35%   18 80%
    19 20%   20 25%   21 c   22 a   23 b   24 a
    25 b   26 b   27 c   28 a   29 b   30 c

Exercise 6.2 *page 64*   1 £32   2 £54   3 £40   4 £42   5 £35
    6 £36   7 £90   8 £80   9 £30   10 £75
    11 £240   12 £30   13 £18   14 £20   15 £18
    16 £9   17 £24   18 £6   19 £3   20 £6

Exercise 6.3 *page 65*   1 £60   2 £90   3 £48   4 £60   5 £150   6 £90
    7 £200   8 £160   9 £240   10 £300   11 £400   12 £100
    13 £45   14 £120   15 £36   16 £30   17 £105   18 £60
    19 £16   20 £36   21 £1200   22 £288   23 £60   24 £30
    25 £4   26 £6   27 a by £20   28 b by £6
    29 a by £3   30 a by £6

Exercise 6.4 *page 66*   1 £45   2 £19   3 £60   4 £72   5 £51
    6 £162   7 £133   8 £375   9 £108   10 £136

Exercise 6.5 *page 66*   1 £40.50   2 £25.60   3 £31.50   4 £47.50   5 £25.50
    6 £112.50   7 £86.40   8 £82.50   9 £199.50   10 £127.50

Exercise 6.6 *page 67*   1 £35, £235   2 £87.50, £587.50   3 £1050, £7050
    4 £210, £1410   5 £14, £94   6 £24.50, £164.50
    7 £31.50, £211.50   8 £8.75, £58.75   9 £15.75, £105.75
    10 £19.25, £129.25

Exercise 6.7 *page 67*   1 £246.75, £36.75   2 £49.35, £7.35   3 £79.90, £11.90
    4 £56.40, £8.40   5 £17.39, £2.59   6 £29.85, £4.45
    7 £97.06, £14.46   8 £33.49, £4.99   9 £27.26, £4.06
    10 £41.83, £6.23

Exercise 6.8 *page 68*   1 +£3.50   2 +£6.50   3 +£4.50   4 −£2.50   5 −£3.50
    6 +£2.50   7 +£3.50   8 +£7.50   9 −£3.50   10 −£4.50
    11 −£4.25   12 −£2.75   13 +£6.25   14 +£6.25   15 +£4.75
    16 +£2.75   17 −£3.25   18 −£3.75   19 +£4.25   20 +£2.75
    21 £1.75   22 £22.50   23 £35   24 £250   25 £3750

Exercise 6.9 *page 68*   1 +20 p   2 +20 p   3 +60 p   4 −£2   5 −£1
    6 −£1   7 +25 p   8 +£2.50   9 +£4.50   10 −75 p

Exercise 6.10 *page 69*   1 20%   2 25%   3 5%   4 30%   5 15%
    6 25%   7 5%   8 20%   9 30%   10 15%
    11 25%   12 20%   13 30%   14 5%   15 15%
    16 20%   17 30%   18 15%   19 25%   20 5%

Exercise 6.11 *page 69*   1 −10%   2 +20%   3 +5%   4 −15%   5 −5%
    6 +10%   7 +25%   8 +5%   9 −20%   10 −25%

Exercise 6.12 *page 70*

1 £800	**2** £200	**3** £800	**4** £500
5 £729.91	**6** £113.64	**7** £120.95	**8** £3829.79
9 £2444.44	**10** £21.72	**11** £2100	**12** £600
13 £1700	**14** £1100	**15** £578.95	**16** £2688.17
17 £1250	**18** £1000	**19** £550	**20** £600

Exercise 6.13 *page 70*

1 £78.79, £450.21	**2** £39.91, £228.09	**3** £187.21, £1069.79
4 £0.45, £2.54	**5** £1.86, £10.64	**6** £3.71, £21.19
7 £14.74, £84.26	**8** £0.53, £3.05	**9** £18.62, £106.38
10 £2308.51, £13 191.49	**11** £1.34, £7.65	**12** £0.80, £4.59
13 £414.04, £2365.96	**14** £2.42, £13.85	**15** £7.15, £40.85
16 £83.40, £476.60	**17** £44.53, £254.47	**18** £78.19, £446.81
19 £44.68, £255.31	**20** £0.12, £0.68	

Exercise 6.14 *page 71*

1 £2700	**2** £4.29	**3** 712	**4** £3000	**5** £114 285.71

6 a £50   **b** £75   **c** £112.50
7 a £28.30   **b** £424.53   **c** 75 p
8 a 25 263   **b** 26 593   **c** 27 993
9 a 50 485 437 **b** 49 014 987 **c** 47 587 366
10 a 2 173 913   **b** 2 362 949   **c** 2 791 763.9   **d** $2 000 000 \times (1.087)^n$

Book 5 Unit 7

AT 2/7 (vi)   Pupils use algebraic and graphical methods to solve
simultaneous equations in two variables.
AT 2/8 (vi)   Pupils solve inequalities in two variables.

Exercise 7.1 *page 72*

1 5, 3	**2** 6, 2	**3** 7, 1	**4** 7, 2	**5** 6, 3	**6** 8, 1
7 5, 2	**8** 6, 1	**9** 4, 1	**10** 3, 2	**11** 3, 1	**12** 5, 1
13 2, 1	**14** 8, 2	**15** 6, 4	**16** 7, 3	**17** 9, 3	**18** 11, 1
19 15, 5	**20** 12, 8				

Exercise 7.2 *page 73*

1 3, 1	**2** 4, 2	**3** 3, 2	**4** 4, 1	**5** 2, 1	**6** 4, 3
7 3, 2	**8** 2, 7	**9** 5, 2	**10** 6, 1	**11** 8, 2	**12** 10, 3
13 3, 2	**14** 2, 4	**15** 3, 1	**16** 4, 2	**17** 2, 3	**18** 3, 6
19 1, 4	**20** 2, 7	**21** 1, 3	**22** 2, 5	**23** 2, 3	**24** 2, 5
25 1, 4	**26** 2, 9	**27** 3, 10	**28** 1, 2	**29** 2, 4	**30** 3, 6

Exercise 7.3 *page 73*

1 3, 2	**2** 2, 4	**3** 3, 5	**4** 4, 10	**5** 4, 2	**6** 2, 5
7 3, 4	**8** 6, 3	**9** 2, 6	**10** 4, 5	**11** 3, 5	**12** 2, 3
13 4, 3	**14** 2, 4	**15** 3, 1	**16** 4, 3	**17** 5, 2	**18** 4, 1
19 6, 5	**20** 3, 4	**21** 3, 2	**22** 4, 5	**23** 3, 1	**24** 6, 2
25 10, 3	**26** 9, 2	**27** 4, 2	**28** 2, 3	**29** 4, 3	**30** 3, 5

Exercise 7.4 *page 74*

1 $x = 2$, $y = 3$	**2** $u = 4$, $v = 1$	**3** $m = 0$, $n = 5$
4 $x = 2$, $y = 2$	**5** $s = 7$, $t = 3$	**6** $x = 4$, $y = -1$
7 $x = 1$, $y = 1$	**8** $m = 2$, $n = -1$	**9** $n = -2$, $s = 4$
10 $m = 3$, $v = 1$	**11** $m = -2$, $v = 2$	**12** $m = 10$, $n = 5$
13 $x = 1$, $y = 3$	**14** $p = 15$, $t = 4$	**15** $m = -3$, $n = 3$
16 $p = -7$, $q = 2$	**17** $x = 1$, $y = -1$	**18** $p = 3$, $q = 2$
19 $s = -2$, $t = 3$	**20** $x = 5$, $y = 1$	

Exercise 7.5   *page 75*

1 $x = 1,\ y = 1$	**2** $x = 1.5,\ y = 0.5$	**3** $x = 3,\ y = 7$
4 $m = -1,\ n = -1$	**5** $e = 9,\ f = 2$	**6** $u = 3,\ v = 3$
7 $s = 5,\ t = 4$	**8** $m = 4,\ n = -1$	**9** $x = 3,\ y = 4$
10 $x = 2,\ y = -1$	**11** $p = 7,\ q = 3$	**12** $r = 0,\ s = 5$
13 $m = 9,\ n = 11$	**14** $p = 2,\ q = 3$	**15** $s = 4,\ t = -3$
16 $m = -1,\ n = 2$	**17** $u = 10,\ v = 5$	**18** $x = 3,\ y = 1$
19 $x = 4,\ y = 5$	**20** $x = 6,\ y = 3$	

Exercise 7.6   *page 76*

1 $x = 2,\ y = 1$	**2** $x = 1,\ y = -1$	**3** $x = 3,\ y = 3$
4 $x = 2,\ y = 1$	**5** $x = -2,\ y = 3$	**6** $x = -1,\ y = -1$
7 $x = 3.5,\ y = 3.5$	**8** $x = 3,\ y = 2$	**9** $x = 1,\ y = 3$
10 $x = 2,\ y = 2$		

Exercise 7.7   *page 77*

1 d	**2** a	**3** c	**4** b	**5** d	**6** c	**7** a	**8** c
9 b	**10** d	**11** d	**12** a	**13** c	**14** a	**15** a	**16** d
17 d	**18** d	**19** a	**20** d				

Book 6   Unit 1

| **AT 2/8 (i)** | Pupils solve problems involving calculating with powers, roots and numbers expressed in standard form, checking for the correct order of magnitude. |
| **AT 2/8 (ii)** | Pupils choose to use fractions or percentages to solve problems involving repeated proportional changes or the calculation of the original quantity given the result of a proportional change. |

Exercise 1.1 *page 1*

1 25	**2** 9	**3** 100	**4** 16	**5** 64
6 8	**7** 27	**8** 1000	**9** 16	**10** 81
11 625	**12** 32	**13** 100 000	**14** 72	**15** 128
16 64	**17** 144	**18** 100	**19** 200	**20** 225
21 400	**22** 1600	**23** 3200	**24** 900	**25** 2700
26 1600	**27** 2500	**28** 12 500	**29** 108	**30** 216
31 256	**32** 512	**33** 576	**34** 500	**35** 1125
36 4000	**37** 16 000	**38** 32 000	**39** 9000	**40** 27 000
41 16 000	**42** 25 000	**43** 324	**44** 648	**45** 40 000
46 320 000	**47** 90 000	**48** 270 000	**49** 4	**50** 2
51 8	**52** 1	**53** 25	**64** 4	**55** 20
56 16	**57** 4	**58** 2	**59** 250	**60** 125
61 40	**62** 8	**63** 200	**64** 2	**65** 1
66 27	**67** 9	**68** 3	**69** 81	**70** 125
71 25	**72** 625	**73** 100	**74** 10	**75** 9
76 27	**77** 25	**78** 5	**79** 25	**80** 4
81 16				

Exercise 1.2 *page 2*

1 a^3	**2** b^5	**3** c^2	**4** d^6	**5** e^7	**6** p^5
7 $2q^5$	**8** $4r^5$	**9** $10s^5$	**10** t^6	**11** $7u^6$	**12** $12v^6$
13 a^4	**14** $6b^4$	**15** $24c^4$	**16** m^7	**17** $8n^7$	**18** $20p^7$
19 d^6	**20** $4e^6$	**21** $18f^6$	**22** s^5	**23** $6u^5$	**24** $35v^5$
25 a^7	**26** $12c^7$	**27** $16d^7$	**28** p^6	**29** $11q^6$	**30** $30r^6$
31 t^4	**32** $5u^4$	**33** $28v^4$	**34** m^3	**35** $9n^3$	**36** $11p^3$
37 $40q^3$	**38** $20d^2$	**39** $5e^2$	**40** $12f^2$		

Exercise 1.3 *page 3*

1 a^2	**2** $5b^2$	**3** $4c^2$	**4** p^3	**5** $3p^3$	**6** $2r^3$
7 t^4	**8** $4u^4$	**9** $3v^4$	**10** m^5	**11** $5n^5$	**12** a^2
13 $8b^2$	**14** $4c^2$	**15** d^3	**16** $11e^3$	**17** $2f^3$	**18** y^4
19 $4z^4$	**20** p^2	**21** $7q^2$	**22** $7r^2$	**23** m^3	**24** $6n^3$
25 t	**26** $6u$	**27** $3v$	**28** p^4	**29** $9q^4$	**30** $3r^4$

31 a^2	**32** $4b^2$	**33** $5c^2$	**34** r	**35** $10s$	**36** $5t$
37 1	**38** 6	**39** 3	**40** t^2	**41** $8u^2$	**42** $3v^2$
43 1	**44** 13	**45** 8	**46** p	**47** $9q$	**48** $5r$
49 1	**50** 8				

Exercise 1.4   *page 3*

1 50	**2** 70	**3** 280	**4** 800	**5** 34.3
6 25.9	**7** 54.81	**8** 25.07	**9** 62	**10** 54
11 6	**12** 400	**13** 900	**14** 1800	**15** 9000
16 723.8	**17** 500.1	**18** 245	**19** 813	**20** 76
21 530	**22** 720	**23** 3000	**24** 8000	**25** 52 000
26 70 000	**27** 5431	**28** 7005	**29** 842	**30** 4350
31 6270	**32** 6700	**33** 400	**34** 32.4	**35** 91.7
36 57	**37** 4.8	**38** 3.7	**39** 6	**40** 45.36
41 53.07	**42** 3.627	**43** 8.005	**44** 0.481	**45** 0.28
46 0.043	**47** 25.48	**48** 78.2	**49** 84	**50** 6.31
51 3.02	**52** 8.5	**53** 7	**54** 0.57	**55** 0.25
56 7.395	**57** 4.032	**58** 0.5607	**59** 0.306	**60** 0.0534
61 0.0829	**62** 3.724	**63** 4.21	**64** 2.5	**65** 0.853
66 0.27	**67** 0.4	**68** 0.035	**69** 0.052	**70** 0.04

Exercise 1.5   *page 4*

1 1.754×10^3	**2** 2.139×10^3	**3** 5.627×10^3
4 4.071×10^3	**5** 3.48×10^3	**6** 1.92×10^3
7 2.5×10^3	**8** 3.9×10^3	**9** 5.0×10^3
10 8.0×10^3	**11** 3.72×10^2	**12** 9.16×10^2
13 4.95×10^2	**14** 1.09×10^2	**15** 2.6×10^2
16 5.8×10^2	**17** 6.0×10^2	**18** 9.0×10^2
19 2.714×10^2	**20** 5.327×10^2	**21** 8.045×10^2
22 3.009×10^2	**23** 4.5×10^1	**24** 9.1×10^1
25 7.0×10^1	**26** 4.0×10^1	**27** 3.73×10^1
28 7.06×10^1	**29** 2.452×10^1	**30** 5.039×10^1

Exercise 1.6   *page 4*

1 53.72	**2** 25.61	**3** 13.9	**4** 45	**5** 416.5	**6** 356
7 630	**8** 2425	**9** 8540	**10** 7800	**11** 10^1	**12** 10^1
13 10^1	**14** 10^2	**15** 10^2	**16** 10^2	**17** 10^2	**18** 10^3
19 10^3	**20** 10^3	**21** 3.512	**22** 5.34	**23** 6.5	**24** 4.326
25 5.37	**26** 8.4	**27** 2.415	**28** 3.57	**29** 6.4	**30** 7

Exercise 1.7   *page 4*

1 1936	**2** 4572	**3** 8126	**4** 5093	**5** 2730
6 9150	**7** 6800	**8** 7400	**9** 2000	**10** 7000
11 932	**12** 156	**13** 819	**14** 405	**15** 630
16 490	**17** 300	**18** 500	**19** 531.6	**20** 495.1
21 107.5	**22** 610.4	**23** 67	**24** 84	**25** 80
26 60	**27** 55.3	**28** 10.5	**29** 94.36	**30** 80.05

Exercise 1.8   *page 5*

1 8.0×10^3	**2** 9.0×10^3	**3** 4.0×10^3	**4** 6.0×10^3	**5** 5.0×10^3
6 6.0×10^3	**7** 7.0×10^3	**8** 5.0×10^2	**9** 9.0×10^2	**10** 9.0×10^2
11 1.4×10^3	**12** 1.5×10^3	**13** 2.4×10^3	**14** 2.0×10^3	**15** 3.0×10^3
16 2.4×10^4	**17** 3.6×10^4	**18** 4.9×10^4	**19** 4.8×10^4	**20** 4.0×10^4

Exercise 1.9   *page 5*

1 56 700 000 000	**2** 567 000 000 000
3 5 670 000 000 000	**4** 1 508 000 000 000 000
5 932 100 000 000	**6** 26 709 000 000 000 000

7 34 500 000 000	**8** 345 000 000 000
9 3 450 000 000 000	**10** 34 500 000 000 000
11 345 000 000 000 000	**12** 481 856 000 000 000 000
13 87 178 290 000	**14** 1 307 674 400 000
15 26 623 333 000 000 000 000	**16** 144 115 190 000 000 000
17 4 727 839 500 000 000 000	**18** 18 446 744 000 000 000 000
19 10 460 350 000	**20** 78 310 985 000

Exercise 1.10   *page 5*   Answers using an eight digit scientific calculator.

1 16 384	**2** 537 824	**3** 410 338 670
4 8 589 934 600	**5** 5 159 780 400	**6** 7.593 75
7 2.143 588 8	**8** 2.660 019 9	**9** 190.049 64
10 4499.8796	**11** 5 764 801	**12** 5 764 801
13 0.735 091 8	**14** 0.205 891 1	**15** 0.038 759 5
16 0.000 000 000 254 629 5 or 2.546 295 E-10		**17** 0.064 610 8
18 16 777 216	**19** 16 777 216	**20** 16 777 216
21 4096	**22** 5.960 464 5 E16	**23** 5.960 464 5 E16
24 9.135 172 5 E17		

Exercise 1.11   *page 6*

1 a £7503.65   **b** £1683.88   **c** £21 477.33 **d** £1605.78   **e** $£1000 \times 1.07^n$

2 a 60 p (to the nearest penny)   **b** £4.64 (to the nearest penny)
  c £20.97 (to the nearest penny)   **d** £16 127.00 (to the nearest penny)
  e £114 232.89 (to the nearest penny)

3 a 3524.7 acres   **b** 3947.65 acres   **c** 6211.7 acres
  d 19 292.6 acres   **e** 2000×1.12^n

4 a £52.60   **b** £77.86   **c** £115.25   **d** £170.60   **e** £252.52

5 a 96 271   **b** 109 749   **c** 240 895   **d** 687 174   **e** $50 000 \times 1.14^n$

Exercise 1.12   *page 7*

1 a £5525   **b** £4696.25   **c** £3393.04   **d** $£6500 \times 0.85^n$

2 a 107.8 kg   **b** 105.644 kg   **c** 99.431 kg   **d** 110×0.98^n kg

3 a 1 840 000 acres   **b** 1 692 800 acres   **c** 1 432 785.9 acres
  d $2 000 000 \times 0.92^n$ acres

4 a 880   **b** 681   **c** 464   **d** 1000×0.88^n

5 a 17 600   **b** 9011   **c** 4614   **d** $22 000 \times 0.8^n$

Book 6   Unit 2

AT 2/8 (iii)	Pupils evaluate algebraic formulae, substituting fractions, decimals and negative numbers. They calculate one variable, given the others, in formulae such as $V = \pi r^2 h$.
AT 2/8 (iv)	Pupils manipulate algebraic formulae, equations and expressions, finding common factors and multiplying two linear expressions.

Exercise 2.1   *page 8*

1 b	**2** a	**3** a	**4** b	**5** a	**6** c
7 a	**8** b	**9** b	**10** c	**11** a	**12** a
13 c	**14** b	**15** b	**16** a	**17** c	**18** b
19 a	**20** b	**21** 14	**22** 12	**23** 18	**24** 22

25 18	**26** 40	**27** 72	**28** 112	**29** 32	**30** 20
31 32	**32** 128	**33** 16	**34** 96	**35** 64	**36** 8
37 72	**38** 128	**39** 16	**40** 40	**41** 7	**42** 16
43 3	**44** 5	**45** 60	**46** 105	**47** 150	**48** 45
49 16	**50** 75	**51** 150	**52** 450	**53** 45	**54** 180
55 125	**56** 27	**57** 98	**58** 250	**59** 108	**60** 270
61 −18	**62** 32	**63** −60	**64** −6	**65** −6	**66** 3
67 −2	**68** −12	**69** 20	**70** 6	**71** 12	**72** 16
73 48	**74** 0	**75** 0	**76** 12	**77** 72	**78** 60
79 6	**80** 6	**81** 12	**82** 12	**83** 36	**84** 30
85 −9	**86** −2	**87** −3	**88** −108	**89** 0	**90** 0

91 a $144\,cm^2$, 60 cm   **b** $144\,cm^2$m, 52 cm   **c** $144\,cm^2$, 50 cm
   d $144\,cm^2$m, 48 cm

92 a $6\,m^2$, 12 m   **b** $30\,m^2$, 30 m   **c** $60\,cm^2$, 40 cm
   d $84\,cm^2$, 56 cm   **e** $210\,mm^2$, 70 mm

Exercise 2.2   *page 9*

1 a £4.40   **b** £7.10   **c** £6.20   **d** £8.90   **e** £9.80
2 a (i) 3.3 kg   (ii) 4.3 kg   (iii) 14.3 kg   **b** 1.8 kg
3 a (i) 5   (ii) 8   (iii) 3   (iv) 11   (v) 7
   b 21   **c** $15\frac{2}{3}$ in   **d** (i) $8\frac{1}{3}$ in   (ii) 8 in   (iii) 5 in
4 a (i) 68 °F   (ii) 113 °F   (iii) 143.6 °C   (iv) 212 °F

   b

°C	°F
0	32
20	68
40	104
60	140
80	176
100	212
120	248
140	284
160	320
180	356
200	392
220	428

   c (i)

°C	°F (approx)
0	30
20	70
40	110
60	150
80	190
100	230
120	270
140	310
160	350
180	390
200	430
220	470

   (ii) when $T = 10\,°C = 50\,°F$ (from accurate and approx formulae)

5 a (i) 5 m   (ii) 11.25 m   (iii) 31.25 m   (iv) 61.25 m
   b (i) 3 s   (ii) 2 s   (iii) 3.2 s   (iv) 2.4 s

6 a

speed (mph)	stopping distance (metres)
0	0
10	5
20	13.3
30	25
40	40
50	58.3
60	80
70	105

b

speed (mph)	stopping distance (metres)
0	0
10	8
20	16
30	24
40	32
50	40
60	48
70	56

c English

Exercise 2.3 *page 11*

1 $\dfrac{A}{h}$ 2 $\dfrac{V}{A}$ 3 $\dfrac{P}{I}$ 4 $\dfrac{v}{l}$ 5 $\dfrac{v}{t}$

6 $\dfrac{q}{I}$ 7 $\dfrac{U}{t}$ 8 $\dfrac{F}{m}$ 9 $\dfrac{m}{q}$ 10 $\dfrac{k}{P}$

11 $\dfrac{W}{d}$ 12 $\dfrac{P}{hg}$ 13 $\dfrac{I}{rT}$ 14 $\dfrac{W}{mg}$ 15 $\dfrac{V}{lh}$

16 $\dfrac{A}{\pi l}$ 17 $\dfrac{A}{4l}$ 18 $\dfrac{S}{4h}$ 19 $\dfrac{A}{3s}$ 20 $\dfrac{v^2}{2a}$

Exercise 2.4 *page 11*

1 ny 2 RI 3 st 4 Lm 5 DV
6 mu 7 PA 8 kT 9 cT 10 $4l$
11 $3s$ 12 $15b$ 13 $10L$ 14 $7W$ 15 $12Y$
16 $60h$ 17 $24D$ 18 $100M$ 19 $1000V$ 20 $50d$

21 $\dfrac{10m}{y}, \dfrac{10m}{x}$ 22 $\dfrac{50a}{v}, \dfrac{50a}{u}$ 23 $\dfrac{25t}{q}, \dfrac{25t}{p}$ 24 $\dfrac{3V}{h}, \dfrac{3V}{A}$

25 $\dfrac{RT}{V}, \dfrac{RT}{P}$ 26 $\dfrac{5a}{qr}, \dfrac{5a}{pr}, \dfrac{5a}{pq}$ 27 $\dfrac{20t}{yz}, \dfrac{20t}{xz}, \dfrac{20t}{xy}$

28 $\dfrac{2V}{hl}, \dfrac{2V}{bl}, \dfrac{2V}{bh}$ 29 $\dfrac{3V}{bh}, \dfrac{3V}{ah}, \dfrac{3V}{ab}$ 30 $\dfrac{100I}{Rt}, \dfrac{100I}{Pt}, \dfrac{100I}{PR}$

Exercise 2.5 *page 12*

1 $u - n$ 2 $z - q$ 3 $t - b$ 4 $360° - x$ 5 $p - c$
6 $n - v$ 7 $90° - r$ 8 $t + r$ 9 $v + c$ 10 $m + z$
11 $x + b$ 12 $n + q$ 13 $z + e$ 14 $A - bt$ 15 $P - qz$
16 $V - ct$ 17 $P - at$ 18 $H - kd$ 19 $y - mx$ 20 $E - rI$
21 $180° - 2y$ 22 $M + nt$ 23 $U + vh$ 24 $H + vt$ 25 $S + mt$

Exercise 2.6 *page 13*

1 $\dfrac{p - q}{n}$ 2 $\dfrac{a - b}{y}$ 3 $\dfrac{E - V}{I}$ 4 $\dfrac{y - c}{x}$

5 $\dfrac{z - k}{t}$ 6 $\dfrac{m + n}{b}$ 7 $\dfrac{r + s}{q}$ 8 $\dfrac{c - d}{2}$

9 $\dfrac{x - y}{5}$ 10 $\dfrac{p - b}{2}$ 11 $\dfrac{360° - n}{3}$ 12 $\dfrac{u + v}{4}$

13 $\dfrac{a + b}{10}$ 14 $\dfrac{x - 3b}{2}, \dfrac{x - 2a}{3}$ 15 $\dfrac{y - 8n}{3}, \dfrac{y - 3m}{8}$

16 $\dfrac{s - 41}{8}, \dfrac{s - 8w}{4}$ 17 $\dfrac{900° - 2y}{5}, \dfrac{900° - 5x}{2}$

18 $\dfrac{p - \pi d}{2}, \dfrac{p - 21}{\pi}$ **19** $\dfrac{t + 5c}{4}$ **20** $\dfrac{z + 7q}{6}$

21 $\dfrac{a - mn}{3}, \dfrac{a - 3b}{n}, \dfrac{a - 3b}{m}$ **22** $\dfrac{p - uw}{5}, \dfrac{p - 5q}{v}, \dfrac{p - 5q}{u}$

23 $\dfrac{u + xy}{6}$ **24** $\dfrac{m + 4n}{q}, \dfrac{m + 4n}{p}$ **25** $\dfrac{c + 9d}{s}, \dfrac{c + 9d}{r}$

26 a $\dfrac{v - u}{t}, 10$ **b** $\dfrac{v - u}{a}, 4$

27 a $\dfrac{E - V}{I}, 3$ **b** $\dfrac{E - V}{r}, 2$

28 a $\dfrac{c + d}{b}, 7$ **b** $\dfrac{c + d}{a}, 12$

29 a $\dfrac{p + q}{n}, 5$ **b** $\dfrac{p + q}{m}, 4$

30 $\dfrac{P - p}{t}, \frac{1}{4}$

Exercise 2.7 *page 13*

1 $2x + 2y$	**2** $4m + 4n$	**3** $5u + 5v$	**4** $3a - 3b$	**5** $6p - 6q$
6 $4y - 4z$	**7** $3x + 6$	**8** $4t + 12$	**9** $5r + 5$	**10** $2a - 12$
11 $6b - 30$	**12** $8 + 4m$	**13** $15 + 5n$	**14** $24 - 3p$	**15** $25 - 5q$
16 $ab + ac$	**17** $xy + xz$	**18** $pq - pr$	**19** $bc - bd$	**20** $m^2 + mn$
21 $u^2 + uv$	**22** $a^2 - ab$	**23** $x^2 - xy$	**24** $pq - p^2$	**25** $de - d^2$
26 $mn + 3m$	**27** $pq + 5p$	**28** $x^2 + 2x$	**29** $t^2 + 4t$	**30** $ab - 6a$
31 $uv - u$	**32** $z^2 - 3z$	**33** $c^2 - 7c$	**34** $4p - pq$	**35** $7r - rs$
36 $8a - a^2$	**37** $5b - b^2$	**38** $2xy + 2xz$	**39** $3pq + 3pr$	**40** $6de + 6df$
41 $5ab - 5ac$	**42** $4tu - 4tv$	**43** $3b^2 + 3bc$	**44** $6m^2 + 6mn$	**45** $4r^2 - 4rs$
46 $7x^2 - 7xy$	**47** $4cd - 4c^2$	**48** $6yz - 6y^2$	**49** $3ab + 12a$	**50** $2xy + 10x$
51 $4p^2 + 8p$				

Exercise 2.8 *page 14*

1 $ab + 4a + 3b + 12$	**2** $mn + 5m + 2n + 10$	**3** $cd + 6c + 4d + 24$
4 $uv + 3u + v + 3$	**5** $bc + 2b + 2c + 4$	**6** $pq + 2p + 4q + 8$
7 $xy + 3x + 6y + 18$	**8** $ef + 4e + 5f + 20$	**9** $rs + r + 5s + 5$
10 $yz + y + z + 1$	**11** $xy - 4x - 2y + 8$	**12** $pq - 5p - 3q + 15$
13 $uv - 6u - 5v + 30$	**14** $ab - 4a - b + 4$	**15** $mn - 3m - 3n + 9$
16 $rs - 5r - 5s + 25$	**17** $yz - 3y - 4z + 12$	**18** $cd - 2c - 6d + 12$
19 $uv - 3u - 5v + 15$	**20** $xy - x - 3y + 3$	**21** $pq - 5p + 3q - 15$
22 $xy - 6x + 2y - 12$	**23** $ab - 7a + 4b - 28$	**24** $mn - 2m + n - 2$
25 $yz - 4y + 4z - 16$	**26** $rs - 10r + 10s - 100$	**27** $bc - 4b + 6c - 24$
28 $mn - 2m + 8n - 16$	**29** $xy - 3x + 7y - 21$	**30** $ab - a + 6b - 6$
31 $mn + 4m - 2n - 8$	**32** $xy + 8x - 3y - 24$	**33** $cd + 7c - 2d - 14$
34 $pq + 5p - q - 5$	**35** $ab + 6a - 6b - 36$	**36** $yz + 9y - 2z - 18$

Exercise 2.9 *page 14*

1 $x^2 + 7x + 12$	**2** $y^2 + 9y + 20$	**3** $z^2 + 8z + 12$
4 $t^2 + 14t + 45$	**5** $a^2 + 4a + 3$	**6** $b^2 + 8b + 7$
7 $p^2 + 8p + 15$	**8** $q^2 + 10q + 16$	**9** $r^2 + 10r + 24$
10 $s^2 + 15s + 50$	**11** $t^2 + 6t + 5$	**12** $u^2 + 10u + 9$
13 $a^2 - 7a + 10$	**14** $b^2 - 9b + 18$	**15** $c^2 - 12c + 32$
16 $d^2 - 17d + 60$	**17** $e^2 - 5e + 4$	**18** $f^2 - 11f + 10$
19 $x^2 - 6x + 8$	**20** $y^2 - 10y + 21$	**21** $z^2 - 11z + 30$
22 $t^2 - 14t + 48$	**23** $u^2 - 3u + 2$	**24** $v^2 - 7v + 6$
25 $a^2 + 2a - 15$	**26** $b^2 + 4b - 21$	**27** $c^2 + 2c - 8$
28 $d^2 + 3d - 40$	**29** $x^2 + x - 6$	**30** $y^2 + 4y - 5$

31 $z^2 + z - 2$ 32 $m^2 - 4m - 12$ 33 $n^2 - 2n - 15$
34 $p^2 - 4p - 32$ 35 $q^2 - 2q - 80$ 36 $r^2 - r - 12$
37 $s^2 - 2s - 3$ 38 $x^2 - 3x - 10$ 39 $y^2 - 5y - 24$
40 $z^2 - 7z - 18$ 41 $t^2 - 3t - 28$ 42 $a^2 - a - 20$

Exercise 2.10   *page 15*

1 $a^2 + 8a + 16$ 2 $b^2 + 12b + 36$ 3 $c^2 + 14c + 49$
4 $x^2 + 24x + 144$ 5 $y^2 + 40y + 400$ 6 $p^2 - 4p + 4$
7 $q^2 - 16q + 64$ 8 $r^2 - 20r + 100$ 9 $m^2 - 60m + 900$
10 $n^2 - 80n + 1600$ 11 $t^2 - 25$ 12 $u^2 - 81$
13 $v^2 - 1$ 14 $d^2 - 121$ 15 $e^2 - 2500$

Exercise 2.11   *page 15*

1 3535   2 8787   3 16 564   4 4182   5 1938   6 5610
7 1339   8 2472   9 7313   10 2475   11 3564   12 5346
13 3136   14 2352   15 4998   16 7350   17 1455   18 2037
19 3201   20 5917

Exercise 2.12   *page 15*

1 480   2 530   3 720   4 370   5 290
6 5700   7 9400   8 3900   9 7600   10 4800
11 9200   12 7100   13 8700   14 4500   15 2700
16 53 000   17 75 000   18 62 000   19 84 000   20 26 000
21 50   22 80   23 120   24 25   25 900
26 700   27 40   28 110   29 60   30 15
31 35   32 300   33 800   34 90   35 120
36 70   37 45   38 75   39 600   40 1100
41 16   42 25   43 52   44 210   45 360
46 540   47 243   48 756   49 31.5   50 64.8
51 126   52 549   53 801   54 54   55 4500
56 3200   57 700   58 860   59 930   60 80

Exercise 2.13   *page 16*

1 $4(x + y)$ 2 $3(u + v)$ 3 $6(a + b)$ 4 $9(m + n)$
5 $7(p + q)$ 6 $2(a^2 + b^2)$ 7 $5(x^2 + y^2)$ 8 $8(u^2 + v^2)$
9 $10(m^2 + n^2)$ 10 $6(p - q)$ 11 $3(a - b)$ 12 $9(x - y)$
13 $7(m - n)$ 14 $5(u^2 - v^2)$ 15 $8(x^2 - y^2)$ 16 $9(a^2 - b^2)$
17 $3(p^2 - q^2)$ 18 $a(m + n)$ 19 $b(u + v)$ 20 $c(x + y)$
21 $d(p + q)$ 22 $m(u^2 + v^2)$ 23 $n(r^2 + s^2)$ 24 $p(x^2 + y^2)$
25 $q(a^2 + b^2)$ 26 $m(x - y)$ 27 $n(u - v)$ 28 $p(a - b)$
29 $q(c - d)$ 30 $a(r^2 - s^2)$ 31 $b(p^2 - q^2)$ 32 $c(x^2 - y^2)$
33 $d(m^2 - n^2)$ 34 $x(x + y)$ 35 $p(p + q)$ 36 $u(u + v)$
37 $a(a + b)$ 38 $r(r + s)$ 39 $c(c - d)$ 40 $y(y - z)$
41 $m(m - n)$ 42 $t(t - u)$ 43 $c(b + c)$ 44 $e(d + e)$
45 $z(y + z)$ 46 $p(n + p)$ 47 $l(k + l)$ 48 $r(q - r)$
49 $f(e - f)$ 50 $t(s - t)$ 51 $m(l - m)$ 52 $d(c - d)$
53 $x^2(a + b)$ 54 $y^2(c + d)$ 55 $t^2(m + n)$ 56 $z^2(p + q)$
57 $u^2(k - l)$ 58 $v^2(q - r)$ 59 $r^2(b - c)$ 60 $s^2(d - e)$

Exercise 2.14   *page 17*

1 $2(a + b)$ 2 $8(c + d)$ 3 $3(m + n)$ 4 $9(x - y)$
5 $5(u - v)$ 6 $12(p - q)$ 7 $2(a + 3b)$ 8 $2(c + 5d)$
9 $3(m + 4n)$ 10 $3(p + 7q)$ 11 $5(u + 2v)$ 12 $5(x + 5y)$
13 $3(b - 5c)$ 14 $3(d - 8e)$ 15 $4(r - 3s)$ 16 $4(y - 5z)$
17 $6(m - 3n)$ 18 $6(t - 5u)$ 19 $2(4x + y)$ 20 $2(6u + v)$
21 $3(6p + q)$ 22 $3(10m + n)$ 23 $6(4a + b)$ 24 $6(6c + d)$
25 $4(2m - n)$ 26 $4(4p - q)$ 27 $5(3r - s)$ 28 $5(8x - y)$
29 $7(3u - v)$ 30 $7(5k - l)$ 31 $2(2a + 3b)$ 32 $2(4c + 5d)$

33 $3(2m + 3n)$ **34** $3(3p + 7q)$ **35** $5(2r + 3s)$ **36** $2(3u - 5v)$
37 $2(5x - 7y)$ **38** $3(3b - 5c)$ **39** $5(2d - 5e)$ **40** $5(4k - 7l)$
41 $2(7x + 4y)$ **42** $2(8u + 5v)$

Exercise 2.15 *page 17*

1 40	**2** 60	**3** 80	**4** 120	**5** 140	**6** 220
7 260	**8** 280	**9** 2000	**10** 4000	**11** 8000	**12** 6000
13 7000	**14** 3000	**15** 1000	**16** 3600	**17** 5400	**18** 1200
19 7800	**20** 6400	**21** 2800	**22** 15 000	**23** 16 400	**24** 21 000
25 9000	**26** 9600	**27** 9200	**28** 9400	**29** 8400	**30** 8600
31 8800	**32** 8200	**33** 10 200	**34** 10 400	**35** 11 000	**36** 11 600
37 58	**38** 72	**39** 34	**40** 16	**41** 70	**42** 90
43 94	**44** 46	**45** 28	**46** 64	**47** 2	**48** 88
49 70	**50** 30	**51** 10	**52** 90	**53** 55	**54** 75

Exercise 2.16 *page 18*

1 $(x - 4)(x + 4)$ **2** $(y - 7)(y + 7)$ **3** $(z - 9)(z + 9)$
4 $(p - 8)(p + 8)$ **5** $(q - 6)(q + 6)$ **6** $(r - 2)(r + 2)$
7 $(a - 10)(a + 10)$ **8** $(b - 12)(b + 12)$ **9** $(c - 11)(c + 11)$
10 $(m - 20)(m + 20)$ **11** $(n - 30)(n + 30)$ **12** $(u - 50)(u + 50)$
13 $(v - 40)(v + 40)$ **14** $(x - 60)(x + 60)$ **15** $(y - 15)(y + 15)$
16 $(z - 25)(z + 25)$ **17** $(a - \frac{1}{2})(a + \frac{1}{2})$ **18** $(b - \frac{1}{3})(b + \frac{1}{3})$
19 $(c - \frac{1}{5})(c + \frac{1}{5})$ **20** $(m - \frac{1}{4})(m + \frac{1}{4})$ **21** $(n - \frac{1}{10})(n + \frac{1}{10})$
22 $(u - \frac{1}{6})(u + \frac{1}{6})$ **23** $(v - \frac{1}{8})(v + \frac{1}{8})$ **24** $(r - \frac{1}{9})(r + \frac{1}{9})$
25 $(s - \frac{1}{7})(s + \frac{1}{7})$ **26** $(3 - a)(3 + a)$ **27** $(5 - b)(5 + b)$
28 $(4 - c)(4 + c)$ **29** $(2 - d)(2 + d)$ **30** $(8 - m)(8 + m)$
31 $(6 - n)(6 + n)$ **32** $(9 - p)(9 + p)$ **33** $(1 - q)(1 + q)$
34 $(10 - r)(10 + r)$ **35** $(12 - s)(12 + s)$ **36** $(11 - t)(11 + t)$
37 $(30 - x)(30 + x)$ **38** $(20 - y)(20 + y)$ **39** $(40 - z)(40 + z)$
40 $(50 - a)(50 + a)$ **41** $(80 - b)(80 + b)$ **42** $(70 - c)(70 + c)$
43 $(15 - d)(15 + d)$ **44** $(\frac{1}{5} - u)(\frac{1}{5} + u)$ **45** $(\frac{1}{10} - v)(\frac{1}{10} + v)$
46 $(\frac{1}{3} - m)(\frac{1}{3} + m)$ **47** $(\frac{1}{4} - n)(\frac{1}{4} + n)$ **48** $(\frac{1}{2} - x)(\frac{1}{2} + x)$
49 $(\frac{1}{6} - y)(\frac{1}{6} + y)$ **50** $(\frac{1}{12} - z)(\frac{1}{12} + z)$

Exercise 2.17 *page 18*

1 3	**2** 2	**3** 4	**4** 4	**5** 2	**6** 3	**7** 4
8 5	**9** 3	**10** 6	**11** 4	**12** 4	**13** 6	**14** 3
15 4	**16** 5	**17** 8	**18** 3	**19** 7	**20** 4	

Exercise 2.18 *page 19*

1 3	**2** 2	**3** 4	**4** 5	**5** 1	**6** 4	**7** 6
8 3	**9** 2	**10** 5	**11** 5	**12** 7	**13** 2	**14** 6
15 8	**16** -2	**17** -4	**18** -3	**19** -5	**20** -6	**21** 2
22 5	**23** 4	**24** 7	**25** 1	**26** -3	**27** -2	**28** -6
29 -5	**30** -12					

Exercise 2.19 *page 19*

1 2	**2** 5	**3** 1	**4** 3	**5** 7	**6** 2	**7** 5
8 4	**9** 6	**10** 1	**11** 7	**12** 8	**13** 2	**14** 4
15 3	**16** 5	**17** 9	**18** 2	**19** 2	**20** 5	

Exercise 2.20 *page 19*

1 2	**2** 4	**3** 3	**4** 5	**5** 7	**6** 12	**7** 5
8 5	**9** 6	**10** 3	**11** 4	**12** 2	**13** 3	**14** 1
15 5	**16** 1	**17** 2	**18** 4	**19** 6	**20** 9	

Exercise 2.21 *page 20*

1 3	**2** 2	**3** 1	**4** 4	**5** 3	**6** 3	**7** 5
8 2	**9** 1	**10** 3	**11** 5	**12** 4	**13** 3	**14** 4
15 5	**16** 1	**17** 8	**18** 9	**19** 6	**20** 7	

Book 6   Unit 3

AT 4/8 (iii)   Pupils understand when to apply methods for calculating the probability of a compound event, given the probabilities of either independent events or mutually exclusive events; they use these methods appropriately in solving problems.

Exercise 3.1   *page 21*
1 0.94   2 0.8   3 0.85   4 0.33
5 a 0.75   b 3   c 7
   d The number of beads must be a multiple of 4
6 a 0.625   b 5   c 24
   d The number of beads must be a multiple of 8
7 a 0.6   b 1   c 48
   d The number of beads must be a multiple of 10
8 a 0.675   b 5   c 81
   d The number of beads must be a multiple of 40
9 a 0.87   b 4   c 26
10 a 0.25   b 90   c 565
11 a 0.000 000 355   b 0.999 999 645

Exercise 3.2   *page 22*
1 0.016 (to 3 dp)   2 0.0036   3 0.000 625
4 a 0.027   b 0.343   c 0.147
5 a 0.008   b 0.125   c 0.03
6 a 0.125   b 0.015 625   c 0.000 455 1 (to 7 dp)
7 a 0.166 375   b 0.091 125   c 0.000 001
8 a 0.1296   b 0.0256   c 0.000 002 56

Exercise 3.3   *page 23*
1 a 0.027   b 0.343   c 0.147
2 a 0.000 512   b 0.778 688   c 0.005 888
3 a 0.02   b 0.72   c 0.18   d 0.08
4 a 0.095   b 0.02   c 0.005   d 0.38
5 a 0.027   b 0.001   c 0.216   d 0.018

Exercise 3.4   *page 24*
1 a 0.008 (to 3 dp)   b 0.292 (to 3 dp)   c 0.175
2 a 0.008 (to 3 dp)   b 0.083 (to 3 dp)   c 0.042 (to 3 dp)
3 a 0.118 (to 3 dp)   b 0.013 (to 3 dp)   c 0.000 18 (to 5 dp)
4 a 0.018 (to 3 dp)   b 0.255 (to 3 dp)
5 a 0.15   b 0.134 (to 3 dp)   c 0.119 (to 3 dp)
   d 0.596 (to 3 dp)   e 0.000 88 (to 5 dp)
6 a $\frac{4}{25}=0.16$ b $\frac{21}{25}=0.84$ c 0.7
   d 0.578 (to 3 dp)   e 0.0017 (to 4 dp)

Exercise 3.5   *page 26*
1 b (i) 0.42   (ii) 0.91
2 b (i) 0.375   (ii) 0.9375   (iii) 0.0625   (iv) 0.625
3 b (i) 0.04   (ii) 0.25   (iii) 0.12   (iv) 0.42   (v) 0.64   (vi) 0.75
4 a 0.25   b 0.5   c 0.75   d 0.25
5 a 0.3025   b 0.7975   c 0.495
6 a 0.36   b 0.16   c 0.48   d 0.84
7 a 0.5625   b 0.0625   c 0.375   d 0.9375   e 0.4375
8 a 0.01   b 0.16   c 0.1   d 0.5   e 0.81   f 0.64

Exercise 3.6 *page 29*

1 **b** (i) 0.46   (ii) 0.91
2 **b** (i) 0.5   (ii) 1   (iii) 0   (iv) 0.5
3 **b** (i) 0.0222 (ii) 0.222 (iii) 0.133 (iv) 0.467 (v) 0.622 (vi) 0.778
4 **a** $\frac{25}{102} = 0.245$ **b** $\frac{77}{102} = 0.755$ **c** $\frac{25}{102} = 0.245$
5 **a** $\frac{1}{11}$ **b** $\frac{19}{33}$ **c** $\frac{14}{33}$
6 0.404
7 0.0435   **b** 0.567   **c** 0.433
8 $\frac{19}{33}$

Book 6 Unit 4

AT 2/8 (vii)   Pupils sketch and interpret graphs of linear, quadratic, cubic and reciprocal functions, and graphs that model real situations.

Exercise 4.2 *page 32*

1	**a** 0	**b** 1		2	**a** 0	**b** 2
3	**a** 0	**b** 3		4	**a** 0	**b** 4
5	**a** -1	**b** 1		6	**a** -2	**b** 2
7	**a** 1	**b** 3		8	**a** -4	**b** 4
9	**a** 0	**b** $\frac{1}{2}$		10	**a** $\frac{1}{3}$	**b** $\frac{1}{3}$
11	**a** $\frac{1}{2}$	**b** $\frac{1}{4}$		12	**a** $-1\frac{1}{2}$	**b** $\frac{1}{4}$
13	**a** 0	**b** -1		14	**a** -1	**b** -1
15	**a** 0	**b** -4		16	**a** 2	**b** -2
17	**a** 1	**b** -3		18	**a** -1	**b** $-\frac{1}{2}$
19	**a** $1\frac{1}{3}$	**b** $-\frac{1}{3}$		20	**a** $-1\frac{1}{2}$	**b** $-\frac{1}{4}$

Exercise 4.3 *page 36*

1	**c** 6	**d** 1		2	**c** -4	**d** 1
3	**c** -4	**d** 2		4	**c** 4	**d** 3
5	**c** 3	**d** 4		6	**c** -2	**d** 4
7	**c** -5	**d** 5		8	**c** $+6$	**d** -2
9	**c** $+6$	**d** -3		10	**c** -1	**d** -4
11	**c** 0	**d** -5		12	**c** 1	**d** $\frac{1}{2}$
13	**c** 4	**d** $\frac{1}{2}$		14	**c** -3	**d** $\frac{1}{2}$
15	**c** 0	**d** $\frac{1}{4}$		16	**c** -2	**d** $\frac{1}{4}$
17	**c** 4	**d** $\frac{1}{4}$		18	**c** $\frac{1}{3}$	**d** $\frac{1}{3}$
19	**c** $\frac{1}{2}$	**d** $\frac{1}{4}$		20	**c** 2	**d** -1

Exercise 4.4 *page 37*

1 4, 5	2 4, -5	3 5, 4	4 5, -4
5 -5, 4	6 -4, 5	7 -4, -5	8 -5, -4
9 11, 0	10 -13, 0	11 $\frac{1}{3}$, 0	12 $-\frac{1}{5}$, 0
13 $2\frac{1}{2}$, 0	14 $-3\frac{1}{2}$, 0	15 $\frac{1}{5}$, 3	16 $1\frac{1}{2}$, -9
17 $y = 3x + 2$	18 $y = 3x - 2$	19 $y = 2x + 3$	20 $y = 2x - 3$
21 $y = 2 - 3x$	22 $y = -3x - 2$	23 $y = 3 - 2x$	24 $y = -2x - 3$
25 $y = 7x$	26 $y = -4x$	27 $y = \dfrac{x}{4}$	28 $y = \dfrac{5x}{4}$
29 $y = \dfrac{-x}{2}$	30 $y = \dfrac{-x}{2} + 3$	31 $y = \dfrac{7x}{2} - 5$	32 $y = \dfrac{-9x}{5} - 8$

Exercise 4.5　*page 38*

1

	A	B	C	D	E	F
x	-2	-1	0	1	$1\frac{1}{2}$	2
y	4	1	0	1	$2\frac{1}{4}$	4

2

	A	B	C	D	E	F
x	-2	-1	0	1	$1\frac{1}{2}$	2
y	3	0	-1	0	$1\frac{1}{4}$	3

3

	A	B	C	D	E	F	G
x	-3	-2	-1	0	1	2	3
y	3	-2	-5	-6	-5	-2	3

4

	A	B	C	D	E	F	G	H	I
x	-2	$-1\frac{1}{2}$	-1	$-\frac{1}{2}$	0	$\frac{1}{2}$	1	$1\frac{1}{2}$	2
y	$3\frac{3}{4}$	2	$\frac{3}{4}$	0	$-\frac{1}{4}$	0	$\frac{3}{4}$	2	$3\frac{3}{4}$

5

	A	B	C	D	E	F
x	-2	-1	0	$\frac{1}{2}$	1	2
y	-3	0	1	$\frac{3}{4}$	0	-3

6

	A	B	C	D	E	F	G
x	-2	-1	0	$\frac{1}{2}$	1	$1\frac{1}{2}$	2
y	0	3	4	$3\frac{3}{4}$	3	$1\frac{3}{4}$	0

Exercise 4.7　*page 41*

1 $y = 10, 5, 2, 1, 2, 5$ and 10　　**2** $y = 12, 7, 4, 3, 4, 7$ and 12
3 $y = 15, 10, 7, 6, 7, 10$ and 15　　**4** $y = 2, -3, -6, -7, -6, -3$ and 2
5 $y = 0, -5, -8, -9, -8, -5$ and 0　　**6** $y = -1, 4, 7, 8, 7, 4$ and -1
7 $y = -5, 0, 3, 4, 3, 0$ and -5　　**8** $y = -8, -3, 0, 1, 0, -3$ and -8

Exercise 4.8　*page 42*

1 $y = 5, 0, -3, -4, -3, 0$ and 5　　**2** $y = 4, 0, -2, -2, 0$ and 4
3 $y = 6, 0, -4, -6, -6, -4, 0$ and 6　　**4** $y = 6, 2, 0, 0, 2$ and 6
5 $y = -5, 0, 3, 4, 3, 0$ and -5　　**6** $y = -3, 0, 1, 0,$ and -3
7 $y = -4, 0, 2, 2, 0$ and -4　　**8** $y = 3, 0, -1, 0$ and 3
9 $y = 4, 0, -2, -2, 0$ and 4　　**10** $y = 6, 2, 0, 0, 2$ and 6

Exercise 4.9　*page 44*

3 a

x	-6	-5	-4	-3	-2	-1	0	1	2	3	4	5	6
$\frac{12}{x}$	-2	-2.4	-3	-4	-6	-12	0	$+12$	$+6$	$+4$	$+3$	$+2.4$	$+2$
$+5$	$+5$	$+5$	$+5$	$+5$	$+5$	$+5$	0	$+5$	$+5$	$+5$	$+5$	$+5$	$+5$
y	$+3$	$+2.6$	$+2$	$+1$	-1	-7	0	$+17$	$+11$	$+9$	$+8$	$+7.4$	$+7$

4 a

x	-6	-5	-4	-3	-2	-1	0	1	2	3	4	5	6
$\frac{6}{x}$	-1	-1.2	-1.5	-2	-3	-6	0	6	3	2	1.5	1.2	1
-6	-6	-6	-6	-6	-6	-6	0	-6	-6	-6	-6	-6	-6
y	-7	-7.2	-7.5	-8	-9	-12	0	0	-3	-4	-4.5	-4.8	-5

5 a

x	-6	-5	-4	-3	-2	-1	0	1	2	3	4	5	6
$+10$	$+10$	$+10$	$+10$	$+10$	$+10$	$+10$	0	$+10$	$+10$	$+10$	$+10$	$+10$	$+10$
$-\frac{8}{x}$	$+1.3$	$+1.6$	$+2$	$+2.7$	$+4$	$+8$	0	-8	-4	-2.7	-2	-1.6	-1.3
y	$+11.3$	$+11.6$	$+12$	$+12.7$	$+14$	$+18$	0	$+2$	$+6$	$+7.3$	$+8$	$+8.4$	$+8.7$

6 a

x	-6	-5	-4	-3	-2	-1	0	1	2	3	4	5	6
$\frac{12}{x}$	-2	-2.4	-3	-4	-6	-12	0	$+12$	$+6$	$+4$	$+3$	$+2.4$	$+2$
$+x$	-6	-5	-4	-3	-2	-1	0	$+1$	$+2$	$+3$	$+4$	$+5$	$+6$
y	-8	-7.4	-7	-7	-8	-13	0	$+13$	$+8$	$+7$	$+7$	$+7.4$	$+8$

Exercise 4.10 *page 46*

1 a 24, −36; $y = 9, 0, -16$
2 a 81, 27, −54, −108; $y = 54, 46, -46, -44$
3 a 27, 3, 12; $y = 2, 4$
4 a $4x^2 = 16, 4$; $4x = -12, -8, 4$; $y = 0, -1, 9$

Exercise 4.11 *page 47*

1 a

d	0	1	2	3	4	5	6	7	8	9	10
$0.9d$	0	0.9	1.8	2.7	3.6	4.5	5.4	6.3	7.2	8.1	9.0
$+1.7$	1.7	1.7	1.7	1.7	1.7	1.7	1.7	1.7	1.7	1.7	1.7
w	1.7	2.6	3.5	4.4	5.3	6.2	7.1	8.0	8.9	9.8	10.7

b

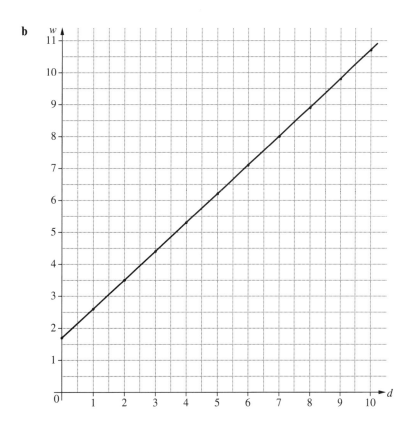

c 1.7 kg
The intercept is the weight of a piglet at birth.
d gradient = 0.9 kg/day
The gradient is the daily increase in weight.

2 a

L	0	2	4	6	8	10
$2L$	0	4	8	12	16	20
$+1.5$	1.5	1.5	1.5	1.5	1.5	1.5
c	1.5	5.5	9.5	13.5	17.5	21.5

b

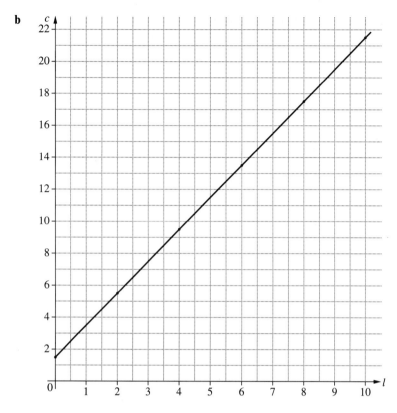

c Intercept = £1.50 – basic cost of an advertisement
d Gradient = £2/line – cost per line

3 a

t	0	1	2	3	4
d	0	5	20	45	80

b

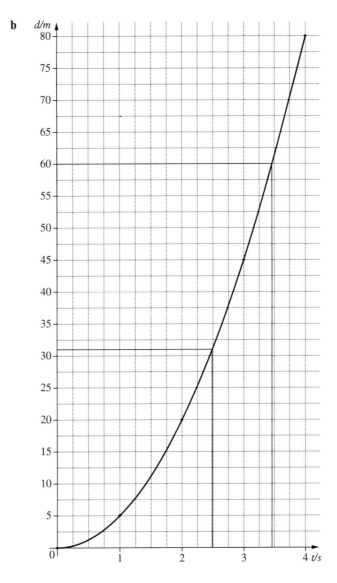

c $d \approx 31\,\text{m}$ **d** $t \approx 3.5\,\text{s}$

4 a

h (cm)	12	11	10	9	8	7	6	5	4	3	2	1	0
w (cm)	0	1	2	3	4	5	6	7	8	9	10	11	12
a (cm^2)	0	11	20	27	32	35	36	35	32	27	20	11	0

b $36\,\text{m}^2$ **c** length $\times$ width $\times$ height $= x\,\text{cm}$

5 b

W	1	2	3	4	5	6	7	8	9	10	11	12
D	24	12	8	6	4.8	4	3.4	3	2.7	2.4	2.2	2

d 9

Book 6 Unit 5

AT 3/8 (i)   Pupils use sine, cosine and tangent in right-angled triangles when solving problems in two dimensions.

Exercise 5.1 *page 50*

1 a 2 and 5 **b** 1 **c** 3 and 4
2 a 3 **b** 1 and 2 **c** 4 and 5
3 a 1 and 5 **b** 2 and 3 **c** 4
4 a 1 and 5 **b** 3 and 4 **c** 2
5 a 3 **b** 2 and 4 **c** 1 and 5
6 a 1 and 5 **b** 4 **c** 2 and 3
7 a 2 **b** 3 and 4 **c** 1 and 5
8 a 1 and 2 **b** 4 **c** 3 and 5
9 a 1 and 5 **b** 4 **c** 2 and 3

Exercise 5.2 *page 52*

1 3 cm, 6 cm, $\frac{1}{2}$ **2** 5 cm, 10 cm, $\frac{1}{2}$ **3** 4 cm, 8 cm, $\frac{1}{2}$ **4** 2 cm, 4 cm, $\frac{1}{2}$

Exercise 5.3 *page 54*

1 $\frac{AC}{AB}$ **2** $\frac{XZ}{XY}$ **3** $\frac{PR}{PQ}$ **4** $\frac{LN}{LM}$ **5** $\frac{UW}{UV}$ **6** $\frac{BD}{BC}$

7 $\frac{ST}{SR}$ **8** $\frac{LM}{LK}$ **9** $\frac{EF}{ED}$ **10** $\frac{UV}{UT}$ **11** $\frac{CD}{CB}$ **12** $\frac{RS}{RQ}$

13 c   **14 b**

Exercise 5.4 *page 55*

1 $\frac{BC}{BA}$ **2** $\frac{LM}{LK}$ **3** $\frac{VW}{VU}$ **4** $\frac{YZ}{YX}$ **5** $\frac{MN}{ML}$ **6** $\frac{QR}{QP}$

7 $\frac{DF}{DE}$ **8** $\frac{TV}{TU}$ **9** $\frac{BD}{BC}$ **10** $\frac{QS}{QR}$ **11** $\frac{KM}{KL}$ **12** $\frac{RT}{RS}$

13 b   **14 c**

Exercise 5.5 *page 57*

1 $\frac{AC}{BC}$ **2** $\frac{LN}{MN}$ **3** $\frac{XZ}{YZ}$ **4** $\frac{PR}{QR}$ **5** $\frac{UW}{VW}$ **6** $\frac{BD}{CD}$

7 $\frac{UV}{TV}$ Q **8** $\frac{EF}{DF}$ **9** $\frac{ST}{RT}$ **10** $\frac{RS}{QS}$ **11** $\frac{MN}{LN}$ **12** $\frac{CD}{BD}$

Exercise 5.6 *page 58*

1 0.342 **2** 0.500 **3** 0.766 **4** 0.866 **5** 0.259
6 0.574 **7** 0.906 **8** 0.996 **9** 0.087 **10** 0.139
11 0.208 **12** 0.454 **13** 0.656 **14** 0.914 **15** 0.993
16 10° **17** 40° **18** 70° **19** 80° **20** 25°
21 45° **22** 55° **23** 75° **24** 3° **25** 9°
26 22° **27** 38° **28** 59° **29** 77° **30** 84°

Exercise 5.7 *page 59*

1 2.828 cm **2** 3.256 cm **3** 1.456 mm **4** 4.386 mm **5** 2.853 m
6 7.368 m **7** 1.719 mm **8** 3.605 mm **9** 2.457 cm **10** 4.17 cm

Exercise 5.8 *page 60*

1 4.854 cm **2** 1.812 cm **3** 1.806 cm **4** 2.472 mm **5** 1.955 mm
6 3.564 m **7** 8.649 m **8** 5.484 cm **9** 2.157 cm **10** 2.464 cm

Exercise 5.9 *page 61*

1 428.1 m **2** 36.0 km **3** 20.5 m **4** 1.9 m **5** 64.0 km
6 34.2 cm **7** 0.69 m **8** 7.3 m **9** 3.1 cm **10** 15.4 m

| **Exercise 5.10** | *page 63* | **1** 40° | **2** 25° | **3** 45° | **4** 60° | **5** 75° |
| | | **6** 70° | **7** 82° | **8** 66° | **9** 58° | **10** 36° |

| **Exercise 5.11** | *page 64* | **1** 50° | **2** 35° | **3** 80° | **4** 65° | **5** 55° |
| | | **6** 76° | **7** 30° | **8** 43° | **9** 71° | **10** 38° |

| **Exercise 5.12** | *page 64* | **1** 34° | **2** 022° | **3** 53° | **4** 19° | **5** 027° |
| | | **6** 28° | **7** 29° | **8** 91° | **9** 29° | **10** 21° |

Exercise 5.13	*page 66*	**1** 0.985	**2** 0.866	**3** 0.500	**4** 0.342	**5** 0.966
		6 0.906	**7** 0.707	**8** 0.423	**9** 0.259	**10** 0.993
		11 0.988	**12** 0.875	**13** 0.669	**14** 0.469	**15** 0.070
		16 20°	**17** 40°	**18** 50°	**19** 80°	**20** 5°
		21 35°	**22** 55°	**23** 85°	**24** 4°	**25** 12°
		26 24°	**27** 33°	**28** 56°	**29** 71°	**30** 88°

| **Exercise 5.14** | *page 67* | **1** 2.427 cm | **2** 5.436 cm | **3** 5.418 cm | **4** 1.236 m | **5** 1.173 m |
| | | **6** 5.526 mm | **7** 4.805 mm | **8** 1.438 cm | **9** 4.312 cm | **10** 4.53 cm |

| **Exercise 5.15** | *page 68* | **1** 2.442 cm | **2** 5.656 cm | **3** 1.456 cm | **4** 2.924 m | **5** 4.455 m |
| | | **6** 5.706 mm | **7** 1.337 mm | **8** 4.635 mm | **9** 6.552 cm | **10** 3.656 cm |

| **Exercise 5.16** | *page 69* | **1** 1.5 m | **2** 9.1 cm | **3** 15.3 km | **4** $y = 2.1$ m | **5** 1.8 m |
| | | **6** 6.9 m | **7** 394 m^2 | **8** 1.1 m | **9** 0.9 m | **10** 66.7 m |

| **Exercise 5.17** | *page 71* | **1** 40° | **2** 35° | **3** 55° | **4** 25° | **5** 10° |
| | | **6** 20° | **7** 60° | **8** 73° | **9** 49° | **10** 38° |

| **Exercise 5.18** | *page 71* | **1** 30° | **2** 50° | **3** 65° | **4** 45° | **5** 15° |
| | | **6** 8° | **7** 76° | **8** 69° | **9** 55° | **10** 32° |

Exercise 5.19	*page 72*	**1** 64°	**2** 37°	**3 a** $X = 18°$ **b** 108°	**4** 37°
		5 27°	**6** 41°	**7 a** $X = 60°$ **b** 69 m	**8** 76°
		9 81°	**10** 80°		

Exercise 5.20	*page 74*	**1** 0.577	**2** 0.176	**3** 0.268	**4** 0.700	**5** 0.306
		6 0.532	**7** 0.810	**8** 0.900	**9** 1.00	**10** 1.19
		11 2.14	**12** 2.61	**13** 3.49	**14** 4.01	**15** 5.67
		16 20°	**17** 40°	**18** 5°	**19** 25°	**20** 14°
		21 23°	**22** 37°	**23** 41°	**24** 55°	**25** 60°
		26 70°	**27** 73°	**28** 75°	**29** 77°	**30** 79°

| **Exercise 5.21** | *page 75* | **1** 2.424 cm | **2** 4.207 cm | **3** 2.66 cm | **4** 1.35 m | **5** 1.95 m |
| | | **6** 3.77 m | **7** 2.5 m | **8** 7.2 mm | **9** 0.88 mm | **10** 0.63 mm |

| **Exercise 5.22** | *page 76* | **1** 4.86 cm | **2** 1.53 cm | **3** 1.224 cm | **4** 1.269 mm | **5** 4.83 mm |
| | | **6** 3.56 mm | **7** 4.9 mm | **8** 0.97 m | **9** 0.63 m | **10** 0.26 cm |

| **Exercise 5.23** | *page 76* | **1** 47.4 m | **2** 4.9 m | **3** 38.6 m | **4** 186.6 km | **5** 1.1 m |
| | | **6** 76. m | **7** 1.2 km | **8** 0.7 m | **9** 2.7 m | **10** 1249.7 m^2 |

| **Exercise 5.24** | *page 78* | **1** 15° | **2** 20° | **3** 29° | **4** 27° | **5** 23° |
| | | **6** 28° | **7** 37° | **8** 35° | **9** 32° | **10** 18° |

Exercise 5.25	*page 79*	**1** 19°	**2** 23°	**3** 28°	**4** 31°	**5** 18°
		6 24°	**7** 34°	**8** 42°	**9** 32°	**10** 34°

Exercise 5.26	*page 79*	**1** 53°	**2** 72°	**3** 25°	**4** 060°	**5** 81°	**6** 55°
		7 27°	**8** 8°	**9** 37°	**10** $X = 14°$, $Y = 34°$		

Exercise 5.26	*page 81*	**1** 63 cm, 61°	**2** 18 cm, 42°	**3** 40 cm, 58°	**4** 22 mm, 70°
		5 14 mm, 61°	**6** 9 cm, 13°	**7** 3.276 cm, 55°	**8** 18 mm, 60°
		9 21 mm, 68°	**10** 6.776 cm, 52°	**11** 3.83 m	**12** 1.41 m